Carmelo Bene (1937–2002) was a notorious Italian actor, writer, and director who inaugurated his theater in 1959 with Camus' *Caligula* then exploded onto the artistic scene with his outré *Christ '63*. Later, he collaborated with Pasolini, Glauber Rocha, Bussotti and others as well as philosophers, like Gilles Deleuze.

In 1983, the fiercely polemical grand provocateur wrote *I Appeared to the Madonna*, a kind of *ars poetica* and chronicle of his life, self-described as very risky, imaginary, and at the same time real. The work is founded on Bene's concepts of non-being, abandonment, and lack. As Piergiorgio Giacchè noted, "the phrase 'I appeared to the Madonna' was never a saying but a doing of Bene's, an event that marked the body of his actor and the corpus of his works: appearing to Our Lady has become an addition to his grace and the accomplishment of his genius."

Less factual autobiography & more autobiographical poem, *I Appeared to the Madonna* tests the limits of lyric versification while its prose, just as Bene's films, is not writing alone but a form of music. This incendiary testament of Bene's life includes tales of his combative encounters with critics, the public, and his iconoclastic views on theater, cinema, poetry & more, including chapters on Salvador Dalì, Eduardo De Filippo, and Jules Laforgue as well as anecdotal elucidations of some of his plays and films. True to Bene's character, *I Appeared to the Madonna* is at once furious, incandescent, comic, and brutally sarcastic; it resounds with beautifully fierce contempt for stupidity and a hallowed view of his own brilliance — finally, fulfilling Dalì's prediction, Bene overcame the suffering of the artist and became a genius.

Also included herein is Bene's "An Autographical Portrait" (the bios has been subtracted), which was conceived as an introduction to his complete works. In this portrait, Bene *rehearses* again his many lives, enumerating the uninterrupted series of illnesses & repeated surgical interventions that frequented his body from his childhood to his death. A body disintegrated becomes a disembodied voice, and all vulgar action (a theater "figure") is subtracted and the lives become works: "What has been disintegrated," Bene notes in his 'Portrait,' "is the concept of authorship exceeded by the deprogramming that occurs in the production and the constitution of ourselves as works of art, of which only the dregs are the object of the typographical body." In this miraculous aphasia-apraxia, Bene's de-mental disarticulation can only parody the unheard song. He listens. With closed mouth. *Sans* author. The inexpressible masterpiece that was, and is, Bene lives.

Translated by Carole Viers-Andronico, this is the first in a series of several volumes of Bene's writings that Contra Mundum will publish. As one of the only true 'spiritual' heirs of Artaud, Anglophones must at last reckon with Bene's genuinely radical transvaluation of every form of æsthetics.

Bène, Carmelo. – Att[ore]
matografico (n. Lecce 193[...
me protagonista del *Calig[...
to una compagnia (primo [...
che ha dato vita a spetta[...
contro il teatro ufficiale si [...
lo e uno stile carico di ef[...
Della sua vasta produzion[...
tra l'altro la manipolazion[...
ricordano: *Lo strano caso* [...
1961; *Amleto* da Shakesp[eare...
stra Signora dei Turchi*, 1[...
Marlowe, 1966; *Salomè* d[a...
beffe da Benelli, 1974; *S.[...
Pinocchio*, 1982; *Lorenza[...
Adelchi* da Manzoni, 1992[...
dei Turchi, 1968; *Don Gi[...

e regista teatrale e cine-
Ha esordito nel 1959 co-
di Camus e ha poi forma-
o in Italia di anti-teatro),
, in cui alla provocazione
iva il gusto dello scanda-
i istrioneschi e barocchi.
eatrale – in cui è costante
integrale dei classici – si
dr. Jekill e del sig. Hide,
e e Laforgue, 1964; *No-*
4; *Faust e Margherita* da
Vilde, 1967; *La cena delle*
D.E., 1974; *Otello*, 1978;
o da De Musset, 1986;
ra i film: *Nostra Signora*
nni, 1970; *Salomè*, 1972.

I Appeared to the Madonna

CARMELO BENE

Translated & with a preface by

Carole Viers-Andronico

Contra Mundum Press   New York · London · Melbourne

Translation & preface © 2020
Carole Viers-Andronico;
*Autografia di un ritratto &
Sono apparso alla Madonna*
© 2017 Giunti Editore S.p.A.
Firenze-Milano.
Bompiani, an imprint of
Giunti Editore S.p.A.
First published under the
imprint Bompiani in 1995
www.giunti.it

First Contra Mundum Press
edition 2020.

All Rights Reserved under
International & Pan-American
Copyright Conventions.
No part of this book may
be reproduced in any form
or by any electronic means,
including information storage
and retrieval systems, without
permission in writing from
the publisher, except by a
reviewer who may quote
brief passages in a review.

The translation has been made
possible thanks to a grant
from the Italian Ministry
for Foreign Affairs.

Library of Congress
Cataloguing-in-Publication
Data

Bene, Carmelo, 1937–2002

[Sono apparso alla Madonna.
English.]

I Appeared to the Madonna /
Carmelo Bene; Translated
from the Italian by Carole
Viers-Andronico

—1st Contra Mundum Press
Edition
274 pp., 5×8 in.

ISBN 9781940625355

  I. Bene, Carmelo.
 II. Title.
III. Viers-Andronico, Carole.
 IV. Translator.
  V. Preface.
 VI. Viers-Andronico, Carole.

2019952614

Table of Contents

0–x TRANSLATOR'S PREFACE

Appearing to the Madonna & Disappearing From the Act
A Brief Note on the Translation

0–45 AN AUTOGRAPHICAL PORTRAIT

46 I APPEARED TO THE MADONNA

- 50 End of the First Act
- 92 Actresses
- 100 Entracte
- 106 Francesco Siciliani & "The Idiots With Flashes of Imbecility"
- 114 Ophelia
- 116 Incomprehension (To Lydia)
- 124 A Prose Stage (Giuseppe Di Stefano)
- 128 Salvador Dalì
- 134 I Appeared to the Madonna
- 148 "Those Who See, Don't See What They See…"
- 164 Eduardo
- 170 Parodies
- 174 "Eusebio"
- 180 From Poetry to Theater
- 184 "Romeo and Juliet" in Paris
- 198 Another One Hamlet Less
- 206 Œdipus the Actor
- 212 To Jules Laforgue
- 216 "Richard III" or on Worldly Crime
- 230 "Macbeth" or the Sunset of Solitude

Translator's Preface

> In memory of Michael Henry Heim (1943-2012)
> A brilliant translator *&* teacher, who taught me
> everything I know about translation.

APPEARING TO THE MADONNA
& DISAPPEARING FROM THE ACT

> "What matters is that we liberate ourselves from language, that we concentrate only on its black holes."
> — Carmelo Bene, "CB versus Cinema"

To say that Carmelo Bene defies classification would be an understatement. As an actor and author, he spent the better part of his life subtracting himself from the tenets and genres of Western representation (i.e., tyrannical, conformist power structures) that he unabashedly despised and ridiculed. Nevertheless, his rather unique approach to creative production, infused with an erudition as profound as it was original in its (re)elaboration, left an indelible scar on the multiple domains in which he (surgically) intervened during the course of his career: theater, film, radio, prose, & poetry — nothing survived his artistic fury.

His incursions into such disparate domains may seem peculiar, if not simply impossible (as he notes in his "An Autographical Portrait," one life was not enough to accomplish all he attempted). The breadth of these endeavors, however, corresponds to a lucid and meticulously pursued path of research into the possibilities — and therefore the role — of every domain of art. Rather than dealing with representations and conveying messages — what Bene spitefully calls the History of (the patronage of) Art — artists should relinquish the constraints of logic & the "tyranny of meaning," offering to the witness-spectator only an incomprehensible and thus incommunicable sound-vision experience. According to Bene, the work of art loses its traditionally prominent role to become no more than an empty vessel through which the artist (the real masterpiece) pierces a hole into the fabric of meaning.

The sundry conceptual devices that Bene utilizes in his unorthodox artistic practices originate predominately in his theater. The centerpiece of these devices is undoubtedly his concept of the *actorial machine* — what he defines as "shredding language-representation-subject-object-History." It is Bene's answer to the conventional figure of the actor: instead of performing a role by memorizing a text and parroting it on stage, the *actorial machine* is first and foremost an amplification of the voice, the aural blow-up, or enlargement, of its dynamics and modulations in an attempt to obliterate the image-representation and reinstitute a sort of natural order of things — as Bene reminds us in his "Portrait": "In our physiological adventure [...] the aural precedes the visual."

The *actorial machine* is also the singular instrument that allows Bene to short-circuit the mechanics of representation via the act. In Bene's lexicon, actor originates from the Latin *agere* (imploring, longing for) & therefore the act is antagonistic to the action (in Italian *agire*, or keeping busy): while the action is what belongs to History (i.e., a chronology of intentions, projects, and plans), the act is the eternal present in which the actor is able to lose his "self." In a trance-like state he sheds the burden of representation, of meaning, and ultimately of identity. The subject itself (as Bene emphasizes, the word "subject" comes from the Latin *subiectum*, or slave) consequently disappears. In his narrative version of *Lorenzaccio*, Bene writes: "History is numeration and nomination; it is the historiography of the dead that excludes me. Alive, I am incomprehensible to History; just as History does not concern me."

Since History and representation are deemed suspect, Bene's theater must become a "theater without performance," where all that matters is irremediably on the margins of the scene (what Bene would call, via a play on words, the "ob-scene"). Hence the importance he accords to "un-staging the play": Bene does not proceed by building or adding; his modus operandi is always that of a surgical subtraction. A case in point is his un-staging of Shakespeare's *Richard III*: as Gilles Deleuze points out in "Un manifeste de moins," what Carmelo Bene excises from this play are all the figures of power. Only Richard III and the women are left, so that the original tragedy, amputated of its fundamental political core, can become something entirely other: an un-staging echoed in the continuous dismemberment and stripping away of clothing and prosthetic limbs.

The battlefield where Bene's iconoclastic furor is on full display is his filmography (& later in television): four short and five feature-length films directed between 1968 and 1973 made to "demolish the image" via schismatic editing, repetition, overexposed sequences, and hyper-saturated colors. An iconoclasm that also explains his interest in radio and live recitations: the written text was for him only a "deceased oral," and reading was to be intended as "non-memory." Forgetting the written text is the only way to resurrect the oral from the tomb to which writing had condemned it.

All the themes briefly touched upon above can be found in *I Appeared to the Madonna*, which Bene describes as his "both real & imaginary" autobiography. The work was first published in Italy in 1983, two years after he performed an unforgettable *Lectura Dantis* in Bologna on the occasion of the first anniversary of the Bologna massacre, when terrorists bombed the city's train station, killing 85 and wounding more than 200 people. Bene was perched atop the Asinelli Tower with a crowd of over 100,000 people below listening to his amplified voice. The book's titular chapter tells the story of that spectacular reading, as well as the events surrounding its mise-en-scène. But *I Appeared to the Madonna* does much more than recount that story: it is a creative narrative that provides readers with the essential critical elements that comprise Bene's narrative, his cinematic *&* theatrical (un)thinking. It is a statement of method, of a philosophy of art and of being, or rather of *not being*, in the world. It also recounts some of his most outrageous escapades *&* happenings, as well as his encounters with the important thinkers and personalities of his generation. *I Appeared to the Madonna* is preceded by the introduction he wrote for his collected works published by Bompiani in 1995 and titled "An Autographical Portrait" (here, the bios has been excised).

Readers will also be blessed with forthcoming translations that will comprise, along with the present text, the prose works Bene included in his collected works.

One such volume will present readers with the novel *Our Lady of the Turks* (1966), which, as Bene notes, is "a perverse novel on the *idiolect*" that portrays a "merciless parody of 'interior life,' risibly entrusted to the third-person narrative form: a monody peopled by a thousand and one voices." The novel was (re)elaborated in images in an eponymous film, which Bene calls "a 1968 film, or better yet, the 'anti-1968 film' par excellence [that was] misunderstood to the bitter end."

Another volume will include a collection of Bene's shorter prose pieces *&* a work for the stage, his version of De Musset's armchair play *Lorenzaccio* (1986), "a study [in the form of a story] on the impossible paternity and coherence of any *action* that in the *act* loses its very intent," which will be accompanied by Bene's short stage play *Lorenzaccio: An Italian Version and Adaptation-Reduction of Alfred de Musset; Italian Credit V.E.R.D.I.* (1965), an "orphaned work" that is "less and more than *an almost-story* of the street market of local *devotion*"; excerpts from *The Voice of Narcissus* (1982), a fascinating collection of reflections on theater that Bene chose to include in his collected works; and lastly, a piece entitled "Theatrical Research in the Representation of the State, or on the Ghost's Performance Before and After C. B." (1990), which excerpts sections of the book *La ricerca impossibile* [*Impossible Research*] that Bene published, alongside a second book, *Il teatro senza spettacolo* [*The Theater without Performance*], during his directorship of the 1989 "Venice Biennale" for theater.

An eventual volume comprising a selection of Bene's plays is envisioned, in the hopes that Bene's masterpieces can be not only read, but also resurrected on stages across the Anglosphere.

These book-length translations are meant to introduce Bene's *impossible research* to Anglophone readers, and the translation project as a whole seeks to incite the reader to follow Bene down his deep rabbit hole. A word of caution: there will be no consolation at the end of the journey. Certainly not a happy ending. But instead of a descent or a fall, the reader can expect an ascent, hopefully a levitation. Like San Giuseppe Desa da Copertino, the idiot saint who "went around the world with his mouth hanging open" and who unknowingly flies, terminating his ascensions in the most improbable of places. These impossible and unrepresentable flights of the Saint are the prime example of what Bene calls "unthinking," which, as Piergiorgio Giacché beautifully explains in his *Antropologia di una macchina attoriale*, is the abandonment that allows the actor to surrender the process of thinking and by extension to shed his identity. It is what will enable him to finally offer himself as a pure vision. To simply appear. Even to, or better yet *as*, the Madonna.

A BRIEF NOTE ON THE TRANSLATION

This translation is not a repeat performance; it is an "other" performance that attempts its own disappearance from the act. While not always successful in that disappearance, it endeavors to stare into an empty mirror identical to the one Bene embodied. To accomplish this translator's task, the translation often employs unconventional syntax and jarring word choices to disrupt the English language and to work on its margins, or its black holes.

To remain faithful to the author's work, and to present Anglophone readers with a similar literary experience to the readers of the original Italian, the translation includes neither footnotes, nor endnotes. There are no explanations given, nor any elucidation provided with respect to the myriad literary, operatic, painterly, and philosophical references from the language traditions of Italy, France, Germany, Spain, and others, except in those rare cases where Bene himself included them in his works. The pleasure of unearthing those references is part of this reading experience.

Bene riddles his texts with foreign words and phrases, which the translation respects, whereas citations that he translated from other literary traditions are rendered in English. Titles of Italian and other foreign works appear in English if an extant translation exists, except in cases where the English title loses a sense that is important to Bene's text. For example, in *I Appeared to the Madonna*, Bene notes the importance of the title of Gabriele Baldini's *Abitare la battaglia*, which was translated by Roger Parker as *The Story of Giuseppe Verdi*. Since the sense of the original title matters to Bene's text, the original Italian is left as is with the English title in brackets.

This translation follows the editorial convention of using brackets to call attention to interventions in the text, which, in Bene's original Italian works, have been rendered as parentheses. Italics, on the other hand, are used for emphasis by the author or to signal a title.

An Autographical Portrait

Talent does what it likes, genius does what it can.

When it comes to genius, I have always been lacking in talent.

Ever since our flowering-fading at the blindness of the light, *the oral has taken precedence over the written*: the written understood as the deceased oral.

The written is the oral's funeral; it is the continuous removal of *the internal*.

From the very moment of our waning birth a destiny begins.

Merciless, for the majority of human beings: if you are not born a millionaire, then you are doomed for life. You must submit to daily life, obtain the incentives for your plan; instead of un-planning, you are damned to the design.

It started when it had ended, like in all "Lorenzaccian" misadventures. Had I been the millionaire Schopenhauer, I most certainly would not have written *The World as Will and Representation*. I would have been very careful not to do so: we are not born to work, to explain ourselves, to think; we are not even born to un-think, because this, too, is to occupy ourselves with thought. We are not born to manage, to acting-suffering: it is all inflicted on us by circumstance.

Just as we passively endure every one of our prenatal perceptions, we will also endure the signifier thereafter. In life's recidivism, the discourse will never belong to the person who is speaking.

The civil registry and the pursuit of our survival condemn us to in-form ourselves, in order to *form ourselves*, to deform ourselves, to become hunchbacks in the manner of Leopardi, in order to play a *part*, when we would like nothing more than *to put art aside*, just like life in general. A real disaster.

Birth is a premature debut, like *Caligula* at the *Teatro delle Arti* in October of '59 in Rome. I had to make my *debut*: it was inevitable from the start.

You are compelled to the breathless *being there*: this obeisance to representation, to books, to this *nourriture* that I could have done entirely without. You cannot escape from the vulgarity of the plot, from the dramatic fart of the State's representation. You are forced to be scandalous, as if it were your "first communion" with an *indifferent* neighbor, with the abhorred condo owner that you will never hate as much you hate yourself.

Being born too early shortens every memory; it is a premature oblivion. *From childhood to the debut*. Since every one of our aspirations blossoms from its ending, we debut badly, whatever the critics may have thought of "*A Star is Born*" in its time. A little like Scott Fitzgerald's most devastating stories, when it seems as though the party, the school dance, was more tolerable, and youth more carefree... That's wrong. Youth never existed, nothing ever existed. Not even childhood, if you remember the endless bleakness in Fitzgerald.

In my first years of Verdian *prison*, the State-*spectacle-of-its-ministry* ignored me and limited itself to arresting me (sic) and not (wait and see) to *neglect* me with lashes from the whip of welfare culture. I would not have become a doubter with so much pensiveness to discard, at the mercy of self-criticism. I would have remained a turd, no longer *disqualified* by the subject's hallucinations, indifferent, safe from *cazzeggio* [dicking around] (an ineffable journalistic neologism, paradoxically approved by those in charge of our news media).

I was not born to be born. Born to work, to be a neighbor, to be a good citizen, having been born without a conscience: having not even been born *to* conscience. I began to act, but not on the plan, on the *act*, yearning for the act... These were things that would come later, after 20 years had passed. We are catapulted into the *darkness* a second time. We are at the mercy of socialites and... we need money. We cannot but find ourselves in *bad faith*. If I had been forced to become a slave trader, I would not have written *A Season in Hell*; I would have gone straight to writing *Trifles for a Massacre*, but not to the (un)pacifying detriment of intrusive popularity.

A good reactionary needs money to defend himself.

It started when it had ended. So, the reactionary looks for the oasis of his very own concentration camp in the "German super-mark": his buen retiro. He is not vulgar like the revolutionary; he has no intention of taking anyone's place, especially not of taking power. He does not want to be a *creator*, an authority, an elite. But he also does not want to be a servant, because "every form of consciousness is servile." If anything, he is tempted by the inorganic. *He wants to be the nothingness that he is.*

Our republic's constitutional foundation is *work*, in any event, preferable to the dreariness of the *job* and *after-work* activities. Therefore, the self-destructive option to make-unmake becomes clear. An inventive plot, this *bitch of a life*.

Once and for all, discarded the dilemma — Moravia was right — of acting younger, intended as *desperation* of non-desperation, every vocation to prostitute ourselves is equally utopian, if not as an *unlived* professionalism. The enjoyment is the *Other*'s privilege (the capital, God. The protagonist is money) as proof of the ontological flatulence between the paying client and the paid whore — *Living Currency* is a great lesson in economics. If being born is *cause for mourning*, being born poor is cause for infamy.

You must work, obligated to churn out one little work after another, and one day you discover that *even* you are an artist, a "maker of farces," a consoler.

Life's indecency tirelessly pursued me from my earliest years. Illnesses of all sorts *&* hospital rooms, continual convalescences; diagnostic clinics: coronary angiographies, biopsies, gastroendoscopies, Gamma scans, MRIs; hospital emergency rooms and operating rooms, bronchial pneumonias, periodontology, dentures, hepatopathies, heart attacks, horrible back pain, discopathies, gastrointestinal dysfunctions, cocktails of anesthetics, fatiguing surgical interventions, ocular dysfunctions, intolerable migraines, irreducible insomnia, urinary tract complications. Not a single shred of flesh escaped Asclepius.

It is from here that a *physiological* intransigence characterized the operative phases of my anti-humanistic research on the dysfunctions and malfunctions in language, annihilating every connivance between the *idea-spirit* and the body that (would) blindly ask to be *disindividualized*, because it does not belong to itself, excused from every motor function inflicted on it by the caprices of the "I," restored to its *inorganic* stillness, vivisected once *&* for all, without any Heliogabalian nostalgia for the "original" unity; gone the body's interior guts bloated to resolve the *discourse*'s rotten meatball — gulped down the indigestible *breaths'* stench — and to chew-disarticulate-expel it in the "expressive" statement of feces and vomit.

Everything is agraphia-aphasia. *Writing* is childish bad faith. The oral is a gurgling cesspit: not at the table where it is in disguise. We disguise ourselves (in jet black, "formal") to "sit at the table." If the discourse does not belong to the person who is speaking, then we are spoken *physiologically*, and the word is an emission of air and the oral lets itself go between two orifices: *mouth-anus*. But when we sit at the table, farting perhaps discreetly, we read the newspaper; we position ourselves with affectation "on the edge of our seats." Reading books is meant for the toilet, without the comfort of guardian angels. The table, on the other hand, affords us the solace of "eloquence"; ornamental art on the walls, tapestries, embroidered table cloths and mirrors, console tables, plasterwork, and "good china"; whereas, in the bathroom, there's always the same toilet paper, which at this point only serves to get your hands dirty (the page doesn't smell as bad as the breath), unless you use a sheet of bible paper (or a piece of newspaper) to polish your butt — whence the universal lapsus of the *Pleiade* in Count Alfieri's bathroom of *stinking Italian mores*.

Physiology is excluded from the novel, from theater, from cinema. There's never been a scene in which the action is interrupted because "She" has to suddenly take a dump... We proscribe anality, the *anal stage*, whereas there is nothing more interesting. On the contrary, we exclude it from our explicit studies to the point that *pensive* defecation, as proud and authoritative as motherhood, preens as aesthetic creation. No musical performance has ever been interrupted because someone, on stage or in the orchestra, was struck uncontrollably by the most natural of needs. An invocation to the *cut*...: "so then, after he had raised his knife to murder her, disarmed by the sudden onset of diarrhea, he fled"; he is no longer a *criminal*, simply because he's about *to shit his pants*.

A plot halted in the aborted act is how I chose to define the *suspension of the tragic*. And like that, thanks to the interference of an unfortunate mishap, the *comic*'s frozen blade turns while piercing the imaginary wound between the risible-shrouded folds of representation in the *theater without performance*. An erotic annihilation.

Eros is the "I"'s raving antagonism. *Porno*, on the other hand, is the *nonreciprocal objectivity of bodies not disqualified by any subject*; objectivity that *exceeds desire, unrepresentable ob-scenity. Flesh without concept.*

The *pathological imaginary's non-History (criminality, transsexuality, fetishism, necrophilia, transvestism* and everything else that is the object of clinical studies in legal medicine) is a much more interesting implication than that of the squalid nature of *everyday life* and of the disheartening grimace of the *symbolic*.

We no longer have time for the pleasantries surrounding existential recreation: for Parmenides, Heidegger, Levinas..., for the *eternal return*, much less for the *return of the eternal*; for the paternal and revolutionary *erections*.

Disindividualizing the body is something entirely different. The therapy for certain diseases starts from the lower of the two orifices. Far from creativity. Disease is a continual variation that doesn't ennoble anything at all. *Pour ne pas s'emmerder.*

The bathroom is the private, the internal. It is the mortification of the written. Expression is the end of the internal, in the arrogance of producing ourselves (*me, the author*), thus every success eventually coincides with the vanity of the debut. There is nothing to sublimate. Nothing. The sublime is not something that hovers above us, like Pascoli's "The Kite."

In any case, *he who does not work does not exist*. Here, it is not a matter of a continuous commitment to eliminate the emptiness of *an existence without purpose*, on which the *world of human work* is based, but rather, it is a matter of being bewitched by that *inhuman* automatism that we call *work without world*.

In this "premature burial," the mass of my atoms deserved, by an unrepeatable spontaneous combustion, an explosion that disintegrated those Scapigliatura *fart-sniffers* of tradition, and those *gentlemen kiss-asses* of the neo-avant-garde who took their early retirement. Even if they fatally keep on re-producing themselves, visibly deafened by the roar.

What has been disintegrated is the *concept of authorship exceeded* by the deprogramming that occurs in the production and the constitution of ourselves as *works of art*, of which only the dregs are the object of the typographical body to follow.

What has been disintegrated is the entirety of the 20th *century*: the anti-neo-tradition's [and Gadda's] "awful mess" which was intended as a funeral service to embellish the eternal sleep of the classics, *&* — in this macabre-cosmetic role — torture-ruin, "unscrupulous," posturing and manners, by tangling up its sense, and by taking scissors to it, pocketing a lock of hair in the "diligent" discord, envious, never tempted to *renounce the sense*; like an avant-gardists' outing in the countryside, far from *ruining the ruins*, at the most riotous hour of recess, cavorting and defacing headstones, inverting flowers, candles, and will-o'-the-wisps, and finally going crazy in that graveyard's mortuary, invoking the *non-sense* and its opposite. Nothing more.

Each day does not contain enough of its own suffering. What did I do, in my many lives? Here is a summary, amply illustrated in my collected works and in the critical anthology that accompanies them:

quartering of *language & of sense* in *un-writing the stage* (paper-oral-musical de-composition of the text)

disarticulation of the *discourse, succubus of the signifier*

un-staging the play (in opposition to the cultish gift-wrapping of "staging the play...")

demolition of the scenic fiction = from the identity identified with the character or from the epic "estranged" denunciation of the re-citing *simil*-actor, who, in the obtuseness of the *role*, disallows himself the infinity of *doubles*, to the furnishing of the *critical staging* like the annoyance of a perm

wardrobe *&* stagecraft-language

radical renewal of the symphonic poem (de)dramatized

the *actorial reading* as a *non-memory* of the *pre-written deceased oral*

a surpassing of Artaud and of the mystical-expressionist *"language of angels"* (Blümner)

the *suspension of the tragic*

the *cinema* as *acoustic image* = *in-con-sequence of the shots* and *the surgical indiscipline* of the *editing*

television neo-technology, discography, and radiophony / a crucial precondition for *amplified phonic instrumentation*

sound samples and *voice re-conversion*

the advent of amplification for the theater (at last)

the *actorial machine* (shredding language-representation-subject-object-History)

the barbaric upset of the '89 Venice theater festival (an institution, based on *statutory norms*, that was restored to authors *&* scholars, and that closed its doors to the audience's and the critics' blah-blah-blah, as well as to that of the institution itself. An unrepeatable and thoroughly documented training ground of *La ricerca impossibile* [*Impossible Research*] and of *Il teatro senza spettacolo* [*The Theater without Performance*] — the titles of two books never before conceived, made available to anyone who would like to take note of them —).

The actorial machine's electronic amplification is to theater what Stirenian *Unique* property is to the History of Western thought.

An inconceivable slap in the face for the millenniums of the *expression-logos-concept*.

The megaphony used by the Greeks is entirely different and rather controversial.

It is important to recognize from the outset the fundamental premise that amplified sound is the exact opposite of a facile artificial limb. An artificial limb is, in short, an "extension" of the oral range, employed for the sole purpose of permitting whoever is preaching to be heard by a crowd exceeding the normal capacity of theaters and public squares; in a similar vein, it is never a sickening reiteration to beat into thickheaded people that utilizing the aforementioned technology definitively rules out every kind of simplistic, electronic manipulation of the voice. Nor can I fail to remind the sacristan vociferance of the State's representation, how the etymon qualifies the *actor* as a *rhetorical-act* of the *oral acting: agere* (which has nothing to do with piddling around on the stage).

At this point, (anything but) a digression is requisite: I have never been able to fathom the foolish idiocies common to the Western nativity scene of parastatal "prose" staging, wherein "actors" and "director-actors" (would) proudly squawk, vaunting the stench of their awful "portato" voices, *stripped* of the most rudimentary amplified acoustics, and all the while contorting themselves — sweaty waiters from Meo Patacca — in cloaks with technological halogens, solarized by electric energy. A ridiculous dichotomy: *zero decibel* (acoustics) and *300 kilowatts* of electrocution (optics). If they (would) vociferate in order to hear and (would) illuminate in order to see, then why on earth (would) they not perform by the glow of candlelight or by the flickering of gas footlights? This enormous incongruity *alone* would suffice to entomb, without hesitation, the entirety of 20th-century theater's vaunted credibility.

Even in the human animal the sense of hearing comes before — and so much so! — its birth: this *coming into obscurity* (far from light). *We hear things there*, in the maternal waters: we are *informed* by sounds coming from exterior (electrical) appliances. We register *passively* clumps of a conversation that does not belong to us (which in the life to come — as I've said elsewhere — will never belong to the subject who is speaking). As for *seeing-there*, we will have to wait several days, once we are in the "world." In our physiological adventure, therefore, the *audio* precedes the *visual*. In spite of the differing speeds of sound *&* light.

In the *non-place* of the *theater* (Ptolemaic representation's definitive closure), it is by no means a simple matter to access the *necessity* of *amplified actoriality* (in fact, no one had ever previously achieved it), at least not without having first pursued in an obsessive manner (subjected, possessed) an *impossible research* intended, indeed, as a *preclusion* to the *possibility* of *finding something*; and, for this reason, it is destiny to have thrown away (to have been... by):

the God-"I," country, government, the State's intolerant tolerance, family, paternity, progeny, the people, History, politics, brotherhood, the neighbor, Europe, the constitution, the civil registry, civic duty, ontology, pedagogy, progress, dialectics, the labor union, the problem with workers, humanism, opinionism, equality, revolution, justice and injustice, social responsibility, actualism, the news, information, liberty (especially of the press), democracy, obligatory college education, optimism, common good sense, the condominium, the public, the private, solidarity, altruism, the race question, the cult of the dead (burying the living), charity, donations, the Jewish dilemma, will, faith, hope, utopia, ideology, the vulgarity of the image, metaphysics, the respect for work, the contemporary, the verb, the meaning, the expression, the pre-written oral work, words, thought, memory, the interdisciplinary-discipline, virtuosity, the blind indiscipline of the opposite of all this.

It is difficult to do justice, in a few lines, to the *actorial machine*'s blinding significance relating to its characteristic *amplified, phonic instrumentation*, as an *audio-visual short circuit* of *language*, with regard to its information-technology use, which is absolutely necessary for all that concerns musical programming: from the individual instrumental sections to the immense symphonic masses, equivalent to an infinity of orchestras (in the laboratory's few cubic feet), to the sound-vocal sampling-processing-conversion; from the auditory *off-stage invisibility* to the oral attribution-expropriation in the *subjects* = *objects* and vice versa by way of the *play-back* (revered-ignored by the actor), in the *unheard of* shipwreck of the roles, ultimately *unrepresentable*:

> (I am) hurting... it hurts (me)... Where?... here(?)
> like a pain that, upon awakening,
> we don't remember...

Here is a body in tumorous metastasis, undivided, since only a deranged attempt might give the illusion of *vivisecting* it, to restore it to the limbs' singularity.

Once the cancerous progression, by this time having spread everywhere, has passed, *this body no longer feels pain in its body (pain to pain)*. The subject is the object — by this point, the dialectic desire deserted —. With respect to the "I": it is the *too late of the interventionism*. In the ob-scene non-time, however, the *too late comes after and before the beginning*.

> Princess, I see nothing nothing
> If someone is speaking to me I Hear nothing

The oral as *a writing accident*:

> And you move your hands
> to spin to spin

> Wools on the spindle that spin other hands

> Red
> a love story that at night
> this one that you say to the sun that it cannot stay

In the de-composition of the *Achilleid* it was my turn (and how could I have remained immune) to share the fleetingness of the oral un-writing: *this role of a desired woman / by a mother all too anxious… in this / …feminine prison…*

> How I said How it was How

The in-sensible dejection of the Homeric hero who was defrauded by Odysseus of his childhood as a girl among other girls in Skyros, and by the gods pierced to this scandal of *invulnerable Vulnerability*. The lost writing's femininity:

> because the heart This does not make me venture
>   into this
> to live among men
> because the heart This does not make me venture
>   into being
>
> (...)
>
> But here there is no return it has to cover me
> Mother
> earth A god forged arms for me
> immortal The arms were immortal
> but horrible I feel
> penetrating flies
> in the wounds of the swarming iron
> worms disfigure the body
> This Life is dead
> This flesh all of it
> rots

I tried to write the *un-saying* — from Statius, Homer, and Kleist — entrusting this *mineral* spasm to spacings, line breaks, hanging punctuation marks.

Exactly the opposite of a "respectable" delirium ("... We hear and we do not speak"), here *a pain is said that is no longer felt*. As Achilles's enamored necrophilia says:

> She must not see you when she awakes
> To this darkness in our women's hearts
> the light of day is a disaster

Instead of as one of Achilles's etymons would have it (*whoever is young dies*), we no longer are, *without never having been before*. In the spotless mirror: where the fable's oral breath (*the saying-trans-passed*) is the last breath from which it dies.

> My Princess bride Princess
> Today was not the day of roses

In my past lives, *automated by alcohol*, I often bivouacked on female bodies: an exercise in "necrophilia," *disindividualized* on the woman's "corpse," learning from it the same predictable lesson contained in several pages torn from *The Voice of Narcissus* and in *Ritratto di Signora, del Cavalier Masoch per intercessione della beata Maria Goretti* [*Portrait of a Lady*].

Like in every masochistic *contract* — wherein it is stipulated that the undersigned is a *slave* to the whims (however merciless) of an actress in furs, engaged ad hoc — the bloodthirsty masculine heat of the Amazonian Penthesilea armed to the teeth with pots, lids, saucepans, and sharpened carving forks — a risible-pathological repression of her own domestic inclinations — is only the polished reflection of *the negation of the will* of feminine abandonment that overtakes Achilles to the point of him feigning having been beaten by she who, a delirious mythomaniac, keeps resounding a metallic crashing of dishes:

> I alone I alone know how to win
> Yes This iron in the sweetest of embraces
> annihilates him on my bosom
> since I will have to embrace him with iron

Forged at the bottom of the sea, this Achilles is afflicted ferruginous flesh, a *Super-actor-machine* obstructed by the superfluity of Vulcan's weapons (the god to whom Homer accorded the longest life: he died at the age of 20).

He has all of its shining stridence, Him, the *bastard* with the vulnerable foot, *almost-immortal*, fully *armored-almost*.

What will this crippled machine ever have to share with his *maid*'s arrogance?

> The coming of woman on stage marks the division between *men and women* once *&* for all, condemned

to sexual characters, different in the sense of differing from one another, effacing *eroticism* on the one hand... and the *obscene* on the other..., the *perversion* that is the theater in its becoming: the *phantasm*. [...]

Here we are again with the couple. So, the *actor &* the *actress* lost *femininity*. [...]

Thus, if in the Shakespearian *Globe* the performance of the *woman-boy* (the present-absent woman) is at one and the same time *nostalgia* and *desire* (*"that which had been imagined / can be un-imagined" at the same time by unreliable playfulness, even in the sinister verses, even in the nocturnal verses*), the fateful revocation of that illuminated *ban* (*of women on stage*) duped both the *woman* and the *actress*, forcing her, furthermore, to take pleasure on stage in what she would complain about (and righteously so) in *life*, by granting her — imagine that — the squalor of these so-called obtuse *rights*, a ridiculous prerogative of the *de-feminized* male. [...]

So, here's a funny one: women would be permitted to return to the stage with the sole, unrewarding purpose — as a *simulacrum* of *woman* — to ward off the *femininity* and the *degenerate* thus plummeted: 18th-century comedy, vaudeville, early and late romanticism of impresarios, real-neorealism, cabaret of emptiness, porno-variety acts, pop music, night clubs; a plot against the *obscene*.

Removed from her *social reality* (...) she is doubly shamed on stage, where she is, once again, confirmed a *servant*: dressed in gold and silver in the heavens and on earth (a *star of the sea* provided that she doesn't exist), a heroine crucified by absurd Wagnerian devotions, she is tolerated as a *redeemer* (*fecal maternity*), forever a victim of *flying men* (*poor woman*): *to redeem is to obey*.
[—"The Coming of Woman," *The Voice of Narcissus*]

The actress. Here is an excerpt from Klossowski's splendid *economic* essay [*Living Currency*], on:

the movie star: she represents only a single factor of production. When the press assesses the monetary value of the visual qualities of an actress like Sharon Tate the day after her tragic death, or calculates the expenses or the maintenance costs of any other woman on the big screen, industrialism itself is expressing the source of emotion in numbers, in terms of profitability or maintenance costs, and thus quantitatively. This is possible only because these women are not designated as 'living currency,' but they are rather being treated as industrial slaves. Moreover, for this reason, they are neither regarded as actresses, nor as great adventuresses, nor even as celebrities. If those whom we are calling industrial slaves here were considered not simply as capital, but as 'living currency' (...), they would take on the quality of a sign of value while, at the same time, constituting the value in its entirety; that is to say, the quality of the product would correspond to the 'immediate' gratification, not of a need but of the initial perversion.

Here's another one [from "The Coming of Woman"]:

(...) Vladimir Ilic Lenin, while watching a performance of *La Dame aux Camélias* in Geneva, wiped the tears from his eyes with a handkerchief (...). What does this mean? It was certainly not Sarah Bernhardt, with her French style of acting, who made Lenin cry; it was rather that Lenin saw in this work, which had always tormented him, what he was fighting against; that is to say, the *exploitation* of man by man. He noticed it immediately in *La Dame aux Camélias* and pitied this woman, *Marguerite Gauthier*, a working-class girl, who is *no longer* a human being, but rather merchandise to be bought and sold (...). I hoped that the Soviet spectator might see how women were regarded in capitalist countries, etc. (Meyerhold)... I would have laughed so hard that I cried twice: the first time for the same reason as Lenin; and the second time because of how *actresses* are regarded in capitalist countries, etc.

But let's return, just for a moment, to Skyros (far from the nuptials in *Themiscyra* or *Phthia*), to the happiness of the *little girl-Achilles* and *Deidamia-"Bea"-"ice,"* wherein the absence of woman is paramount.

> What is a *little girl*?, to start with, what is she not. She is not a woman. She is lovely because *she is not. The woman is. And it is anything but "wonderful."* [...]
>
> A little girl as a female in miniature is *vulgar*...
>
> A little girl, *unconscious providence of omnipotence*, is a miracle, because, even though not quite a woman in our eyes, she is real and alive. (*She is*) a *work* of art. [...]
>
> *Every* dongiovannism *is "leporello": this villainous way of joking — an insult to the game —* with grown women, who unfortunately, exist, who encumber, who have ceased not being, and who are no longer that which we lack... A little girl is an innocent and perverse game. Mozartian. Little girls are Mozart's notes... Life is a little girl, and that's all; blond hair, blue, green, black or violet eyes...

... Anyone who embraces an (adult) woman is a miserable wretch...

To flinch at "*Bea*" and "*ice*." It is the aphasia of nomination. The word missing in *Beatrix* (in happiness).

If the word is a gift in the mouth for someone who does not use it to say something other than the word itself, then what will *losing the power of speech* ever mean.

Here we have Schopenhauer, the *teacher*, turning away from Raphael's painting: Saint Cecilia (*blind*), blessed, is removed from her musical instruments and carried off by actual angels on high, beyond the canvas:

> What does she do with the angels' harmonies, when she has found the angels.

[...] An absent woman = a little girl: a lost word, that *in the saying falters*... It is *the voice* that *loses itself*.
[—"Life as a Little Girl," *The Voice of Narcissus*]

The male-woman exhausts herself in carrying the burden of *fucking*, ignoring *copulation* as a *surrogate* for *masturbation*; and, what's more, the woman is *unaware of the orgasm* that she experiences (endures). The mystic list includes a multitude of women who cannot (do not know how to) *tell us anything* about their *raptures*. Angela da Foligno's writings are a disappointment in *every sense*; a recidivist omission of her pathological devotions. The blessed saint would kneel and apply herself, among other things, to collecting — with her pious hands — the purulent pus and flakes of scabs from the sores on lepers' arms and legs in a washbasin and then gulping down all that fetid and infected matter.

We find no trace, however, of these exaltations in her inane catechismal "diary."

A spiteful enemy of every *infantile* and *individual* game (even when she feigns, childishly unconscious, some sort of aesthetic interest), woman remains a *servant-soubrette* of social-worldly excrement, naturally a servant subjugated to the quotidian caprice of the *plebs' tyranny*.

Actress. Actor-actress without a *double*, in the *role* of roles *without a game*, in the perpetual search for the "author," who superimposes the identity of a second mask (the *role*) on the *identico* of the original mask: the "nude" tights in that dimwit Pirandello's work.

> My contempt for today's actor lies here: in his highly sought-after *simulation*, in his panhandling for a miserably believeable performance;

in his inability, at this point far too proven, to put at stake anew *the very method of doing theater* at every performance; in his idiotic terror of self-marginalization; in his tedious blathering about the "theater in crisis" and, therefore, having never been tempted enough by the waltz of a *theater of crisis*; in his exclusively *masculine* method (if we could even call such a pitiful constraint a method).

[— "The Coming of Woman," *The Voice of Narcissus*]

Beyond the, at this point established, discourse on the *deficiency* of woman (feminine absconding) that condemns her to the role of an ir-responsible creator of *human excrement*, and to the indecent splendor (comparable to the *worker's narcissism* in the Deleuzian metaphor for "popular theater") of a socialite *actress* who is indisputably precluded from the *actorial machine*'s function..., womanly *stupidity* is beastly disenchantment, thoughtless and deranged lightness in her inconstancy.

> If extended it hurts
> this hand if it wants
> to hold by the strand of golden hair
> the glory if it brushes against me
> the Black force no longer wanting the foreign gesture

Such a feminine psychosis can come, however, to the aid of a Sacher Masoch and, in the same vein as president Schreber, persuade him, delirious-involuntary, to renounce that ever pensive *virile "I"*'s narcissistic humor, to dampen its exhausting perversion, to entomb the dusty and austere tail-coat of the retired appellate court president, in order to undergo a therapy that is unthinking, unconcerned, and that makes womanly humors fade away:

> (...) "You poor thing, it's not enough... for thinking of nothing! It's simply not enough. Look at me. You wrote me. If I escaped from your pen, then why don't you believe me? Why do you persist in reading and re-reading this mistake that is bigger than you are? Tear up your mediocre assignment in a thousand pieces, in a thousand little senseless assignments... Believe me, and I'll be another one who is not. You'll think of me among the angels, among the infinite azure figures of speech that we don't think about anything! (...) It's a matter of skin. Leave profundity to the men, between one toothache and another, the miserable wretches! When a respectable woman finds a nice pair of silk stockings, she can't wait to put them on. She's no longer herself, with how well they suit her! She's wearing silk!... But there's no guarantee that they'll fit you. Perhaps — you need only try them on — your

carefreeness is made of cotton. Who knows, maybe it's velvet. Perhaps yours is a mid-season tranquility. You just have to try... (...) Why do you answer me? Why do you explain yourself? And shouting to boot? 'Recently, I found,' that's more than enough! You can keep the end of that sentence to yourself, you poor man! A real woman couldn't even think of how to finish that sentence! Dammit!... Ah ah ah! You're asking yourself 'who are you saying dammit to,' aren't you? Ah ah ah, I don't even know myself! I don't know a damn thing! But if it makes you happy, I can add: 'Dammit to that whore of a seamstress of mine; if I run into her, I'll tear out her eyes!'... But I assure you, the thought never crossed my mind. You poor man!"

(...) ... Alas!, you poor man... You see, alas!, even in this simple relationship, you can see that you are unable to become an idiot... alas!, you won't get forever distracted...

(...) ... Come here, come here, let's rummage around together. The shoes I was wearing yesterday, the white ones, they're too small for you. Come here, it isn't anything so transcendental: it's only a question of size, of numbers, of the cut, and nothing more...

(...) It's fine, nothing to worry about. Up 'til now you had hoped to humiliate yourself with the sole purpose of driving yourself crazy. And to drive yourself crazy, you needed a woman. Now, you can simply lose your head. You're not crazy for her anymore, you know? Just crazy, and that's all! Disappear completely!? Why not, at this point?... You see, you can talk nonsense without feeling any pain. Dress in tailored clothes. Ladies only go crazy when they dress well, otherwise they may as well remain men... You shouldn't follow my example: you want to survive. Mine was a passion in costume. Devote yourself to me. Devoted, not sanctimonious. You only have to believe in the nothingness that you are not! Appearing; when someone appears, we immediately say that he is not. We say that he is not what he appears to be to us... Isn't that what you want? It's the only way to not be in the world! Appearing! The pansies of thought... Extravagance, no! We can't go around wearing a costume and survive! (...)

[—*Portrait of a Lady*]

So, under so much luminous rain from thoughtless fireworks, the "professor" is finally ready to trade his *tenure* for *indecency*, the *boots-testicles & the academic decorum* for the *disguise & the aphasia*; to shod-clothe — enraptured, in a designer's studio — his partner's shoes, intimate garments, and clothes, testing, in the fabric's style-color-quality, the enchanted variety of the mood's contrasts that overtakes and excites him, and which is therefore not suitable for that forgetful aged peace to which he aspires:

> (...) No impatience, do you hear me? Now you know that other men, other women, trains that go by also exist... You will have to work together... actually, let's put it this way: it's the others who will have to work with you, so that you exist, so that you are a woman alone at last, tranquil and carefree. Amuse yourself only by playing the piano. Playing a little piece of life for me. We'll sing, if you like, but without following the music at all; as if, instead of being in this room, we were in the other room, entirely elsewhere... as if we were no longer us. And, above all, we will not work — do you hear us? — We will not work. And we will never be able to die!... Children? Perhaps. One day, when God will be worthy of them... You create humanity just to have something to do... It's weird, so very weird!... ... Naturally, some of that male hairiness remains... a moderate amount, for that matter... It's weird... the nipples... the nipples... Weird... very weird... ...Very weird! Am I planning to go on a trip?... Ah ah ah... I'm about to go into a rapture! ... Of course, I'm about to shit my pants... (...)

(*wearing a somber grey pants suit and a hat with a veil*)

This man is a lady
indisposed
indisposed to the extent that it's not an affair
It's not an affair of men
Much less an affair for lonely men
I'm about to shit my pants... At last...

I am a lady
For that modicum of respect that I deserve
Since I leave the affair to men
to workers
to men's fashion
To evacuate my bowels
Without Marys messing about in the house
without nurses for love of the law
Evacuatesocialdemocracy
I'm about to shit my pants
To live as a couple As a family...
Living as a family is a catastrophe...
always occupied... That's grace...
That's grace
Until now, I hadn't deserved
to find the bathroom unoccupied.

[*—Portrait of a Lady*]

It is very difficult to translate to the stage the preceding passage from *Ritratto di signora di Sacher Masoch* [*Portrait of a Lady by Sacher-Masoch*] (not following De

Musset's example of *Armchair Theater*), because it is fatally destined to typographical *bodies* and forbidden to actorial bodies. This material is *literally* unrepresentable for the simple (and extremely unfair) reason that the penal code does not allow anyone to tear *an actress* into a million pieces with impunity.

Whoever reads my work has undoubtedly understood that, especially in my "digressions," I have never let up, not even for a minute, on the urgency of the *actorial scandal* that is the *language-shredding machine*.

To provide an additional, very clear audio-visual exemplification of the *amplified actorial machine*, I now propose a synthesis-collage of *Lorenzaccio*, which appears as the first piece in my collected works. This piece is a little miracle, in my opinion, that no protracted critical essay would ever be able to produce:

> Lorenzaccio is the very gesture that in its accomplishment disapproves. It disapproves of the acting. And the Medicean History, dispensed with, does not, in fact, know how to tamp this its (?) heroic enigma; this History bore *&* glorified far worse than that. So there are two possibilities: either History, along with its imbecilic cult, is an imaginary writing exemplary of the infinite possibilities excluded from the arbitrary arrogance of the "events"

that took place (infinity of the aborted events); or it is, rather, an inventory of events without authors, generated, that is, from the unconsciousness of the respective actors (because a void in memory is needed for an action to occur) that in the execution of the project, suspended in the void of their long-chased and wearied dream, driven mad, they would lose that very project along the way, (un)fulfilling it completely. Carthusian in their patient, intense labor of tracing the plot of the preparations, prudent, meticulous, feverish from the unmentionable anguish, from the insomnia of the being there — the intolerable inhuman omnipresence of the self to oneself — they would precipitate in the moment an entire thoughtful life: the gesture. And they were no longer. For a moment. They are excluded from enjoying the emptiness of unending, unlivable happiness; to awaken just after, newly overwrought & unhappy, wearing gypsy masks on horseback — whether tourists or exiles — on their way to the putrid waters of Venice, the thermal city of our century for those who wish to die.

(...) In that nocturnal scrap of the History of art, from the heights of his dwelling on Via Larga, at the hour when the Florentine copies were sleeping, dreamed up by the simulacrum that might recreate them, Lorenzino defied the deafening silence, because the gestures, the footsteps, the documents on ancient Rome he was rummaging through, and his whispered commentary on those anecdotes seemed to him extraordinarily amplified; it was as if in the room, in the other room, the heroic empty shell of a suit of armor was doing its best, like a sound-effects expert, to dub those ordinary actions with perfect synchronicity, however unsettling that might be. The modest, meaningless deafness of that utterly bewitched housework unwittingly adorned itself with the epic's resonance: the pages clicked metallic, the fluids flowed into flutes with the roaring of alpine falls, the porcelain and the pewter, by simply touching the surfaces, exploded into dark and alarming fireworks, and the phonemes, the Lorenzian phrases, only hinted at, seemed to be broadcast at an excessive volume. All of it resounded in the silence as if there were a grumpy giant bustling about in a kitchen somewhere. Did Lorenzino really hear that racket, or was it only in his head?

(...) We will call him Contini, that giant non-existent warrior, a deafening sound-effects expert of Lorenzaccian gestures. In the economy of an Italian theater space, this empty armor at the center of his amplified devices, if visible, would operate in the pit usually occupied by the orchestra, euphemistically known as the mystical gulf. Contini is not Lorenzo's double, because he performs with his back to the stage. The racket he makes has no meaning; it's an historical racket and nothing more; just like the hypothesis of a crazy signifier is entirely at the hazard of the spectator. Contini performs, amplifying the Lorenzaccian movements, the Lorenzaccian steps, displaying in them both synchronicity and asynchronicity, but for himself alone; his will an end in itself, dispossessed of any sort of common sense: he drinks, he breaks plates, glasses, and so forth into the microphones. A sixteenth-century, empty-shell warrior is in every way similar to a sound-effects expert immersed in the darkness of a cinematographic audio dubbing room; a pro in producing his "effects," with only this difference: he has his back to the image.

Lorenzaccio (...) was roused by a deafening, indecipherable noise, as if an armored body crashing on the marble floor somewhere, and from a voice that was his own (had he said something?), this too, amplified. Had Contini bumped into something? And Lorenzo, what on earth had he said? At this point, it was incredible, his self-consciousness as an actor was incited by the vocational idiocy of ham actors when their jokes fall flat: he did all he could to make up for his double delay by articulating, like a fish in a veiled hat's aquarium, the nothingness of the already spoken (unacceptable play-back), and by immediately knocking over a laid table (which one?), a deaf-mute effect, since the objects flaked to the floor like snowflakes in a nightmare. He was assailed by the ridiculousness of the desolate failure of this simulated syntony, and his shame prompted him to disappear, down there, between the legs of his writing desk.

Crouched in this manner, uncomfortable even, Lorenzaccio had the opportunity to think back on that incident. Had he been so late, preceded, that is, by his own gesture?

(...) So this is how every project is mortified. Why then this great journey, if its intent blossoms from its outcome?

(...) He got up suddenly, hurled insults at the objects around him: the porcelain, the pewter, the Latin edition of *Plutarch's Lives*; an arbitrary rain on the rug, but soundless; neither synchronous nor asynchronous: soundless. Was he not the author of this insipid, small catastrophe?

[...] Contini, who had perhaps recovered from the incident (if it had ever happened), now seemed to have gone mad, judging from the deafening autonomy of the racket he was making. The amplified sounds preceded the Lorenzaccian gestures.

A Narcissus without voice *&* without image, Renzino was at the mercy of becoming. He was moving about in a film that was so asynchronous that another actor "in his place" would have left the stage without the slightest hesitation. He was so late in his gestures, cold, insignificant, that the sound exploded, preceding him, but of its own accord, gratuitous and unpredictable.

(...) Lorenzaccio adopted, perhaps, the stupidest of solutions: as if on the stage at the mercy of the Florentine copies, he tormented himself by following in his own footsteps, in his own movements, and in his own hesitated gestures which were produced by the resonance, *vainly seeking to reduce the interval of his already intolerable lateness.*

Always with his back turned to the Medicean image, Contini consumed his "crazy tea" into the microphones; and Lorenzino, behaving like an idiot, wriggled about — we might have said — to second him. This wasn't really the case, but it seemed to be, or it could have seemed that it was. If, for example, he heard the amplified sound of a plate shattering on the marble floor, he would grab the closest object at hand and fling it onto the deaf rug: he deluded himself by thinking that in this way he reduced the delay (fractions of seconds counted), and, in this way, he recounted it to who knows whom.

He seconded what had already been done, what had already happened (in his mind, elsewhere) to remain on stage at all costs. What an incredible film it would be if the filming of the images followed the dubbing.

(...) Meanwhile, Contini unsheathed a large blade, between hurling rocks into the Venice buckets and rolling huge balls of yarn on the wooden platform that resounded with the sinister grumbling of a storm; and, in the midst of the crashing sounds from the bad weather repertoire, he showed himself by taking great leaps while swinging that heavy, hissing weapon, grasping it with two hands and shouting at the nothingness. And that poor woman that was Lorenzaccio, who felt faint at the very idea of a duel, was obliged all the same to take note of the enormity of the delay on that sonorous gesture (which one?) that was, nevertheless, "his own," on the expropriated ferocity for which he was responsible. Reanimated by the game's necessities, Lorenzino emerged from under the rug and, having invented a feather-duster from the surface of an ironing board (the museum was occasionally used for temporary fashion shows), he grasped it as if it were a fencing foil, and stupidly hopped around on what had happened.

Then, surprised by another sound, he seconded the gesture beforehand by moving around some of the random objects on the tables and on the floor, and by smashing others with an accuracy that was increasingly clumsy. Is this not perhaps how we dispose of ourselves? Resonance is the first intent, and the body that imitates it is the elderly satisfaction of a hobbling grandfather who follows his grandchild into a game free from the shadow of what was and what will have been. Lorenzaccian acting is to disregard the intent itself, not to prevent it from its outcome, take note, but to second it, second in any case; the act has neither minutes nor seconds because *it does not take place* in the actor's world. The actor is out of place in his breathlessness.

So that's it. I haven't really succeeded in avoiding this d'après of the "lorenzaccio" portrait, reproduced here, I repeat, with the sole purpose (hopefully efficacious) of a reading-performance of the *actorial machine's phonic amplified instrumentation*.

Throughout my first decade in theater, I appeared on stage without so much as a microphone cable, *as if* I were equipped with a *phonic amplified instrumentation* that would come later, and by exploiting the very same oral constants of an elemental, fundamental research: the *verticality* (meter *&* prosody) of the *verse* (and of free verse), the internal stresses in the *prose poem*, the *closed* voice (from the Gregorian chants to the polyphonic *lied*, against the vibrato of the bel canto), *the spoken parts in opera*, the musical *intention*, the *dynamics* and the *(de)modulations* of *frequency* in the diaphragmatic contractions, the sparsely scrutinized *cure for defects*, the *amplitude* of the *timbre's range* and *tonal variations*, the *staccato*, voice production (chest-mask-head-palatal), etc., but while always forcing pitches and peaks *within* the *harmonic band*'s and the always engaged *basso continuo*'s monotonous chart (to adorn the sound with a halo); the inhalation and holding the breath, the vocalic leap exasperatingly outlined to unnerve the phrasing of the logos (a syntactical mishap ever since the first edition of *Pinocchio*): whence that *magical reciting on ourselves* that didn't escape the notice of the most perceptive of listeners.

This "pre-amplified" training ground was essential, like in a *wide shot*; at times even less: something closer to an (un)articulated delirium behind crystal.

Nevertheless, such a *lens* for an "oral optics" in a *wide shot* was not enough to create an *implosion* capable of definitively *extinguishing* the *voice*; albeit "behind crystal," we were perceiving, even if minimized from a distance (the distance between who is speaking and who is listening) a little draft of the *subject* (however crouched over he may be) who was *vomiting*, yes (he was *vomiting on himself*) the text *in clumps*, but, in his *proffering-wounding* his insides, he wasn't able to *nullify* the perception of speaking in those who were listening to him.

All this to say that the audience was hearing me *a little too much* in the theater. A bit like how an *inconceivable* "breath" is clumsily preceded by a prompter's hyper-articulated scansion. Or, in the heart of the night, in certain hotel rooms, even if muttering something to oneself, we are hushed by the guests in the neighboring room; the other guests' annoyance is more than understandable, since they are annoyed by the insignificance that they can barely hear (if bothered by a shouting match they can understand, they are likely to be furious): in both cases, the guests are being disturbed by squabbles that don't *interest* them. Unless, of course, that murmuring-shouting is not a gurgling of *their own* stomachs; that is to say that this noise *resonates within* them. In this case, it is *their own* internal disturbance (without any mediation of listening) that is as *vital* as it is *intolerable*.

In any event, it would be a good idea to soundproof all of the rooms in this hotel: so that we can murmur — we who read distractedly, sleepy *&* forgetful, and the guests who don't feel well (each of us in our own rooms) abandoned, but in the *same* our-their *unheard* ventriloquy.

The audience was hearing me *a little too much* in the theater. Too little; worse: discreetly.

To nullify the "drafts" of the logos and of its conceptfull usage, we simply (!) needed to *wall* the "fourth wall." Make it impervious to flights *of* sense. Wall it against the gossipy misunderstandings of the listening in the contagious flatulence of the *being* (*there*).

If — here's another example — we are observing, from a distance, a painted image (whose formal material may even be a work of art *in the making*), we are nevertheless unable to critically resign ourselves: to not (ad)miring it as *thinking* subjects, as if it were inscribed in a proscenium. If we approach this figuration, then we give up, little by little, the totality of its vision, followed by its peripheral details, until all we see is a blurry detail in extreme close-up. If we were to go so far as to brush our nose against the surface, then it would be as if we had shut our eyes tight to block out that vision. This *darkness of everything* is tantamount to the summit of *acoustic enlargement*.

The *maximum* volume (phonic level), however, of electronic amplification corresponds to its *minimum* auditory emission, since, once all mediation has been cut, the *voice's energetic dynamics burn only in the interior* (of he who speaks and of he who listens), disindividualized and *unheard, unprovable*.

It is the phenomenology of the subject that fades away, in the basso continuo's *blind will*, just like the solarization of a pre-written text and of its representation, & the liquidation of language and of its History.

The *lyric*'s verticality, irreducible to thought, crucified on the *epos*, short-circuits any desire for listening. *Inconceivable*. Without a trace.

The actorial *reading*'s (dis)concert is pure *resonance beyond* the *forms*; no longer re-cognizing any text, it is the *amnesia* of the deceased oral's written, dispossessed of its own emission of voice, even from the body, subtracted from the master's virtuosity, and — abandonment's orphic grace — from the artistic misery of the expression that is physiologically *expelled* by the *disappearance* of the actorial corporality.

Before and after the History (of the patronage) of art in its adorned, consolatory hypocrisy, before and after its kaleidoscopic social entertainment, *actoriality* is ultimately *extraneous to its own production*: vocality dressed-up with reverberation. This can only be understood by he who has been visited, who knows where, by this *elsewhere* of the *aesthetic must-not-be* that severs the (no longer his own) flow of the producing-articulating ourselves in a *work of art*. Masterpieces don't exist.

Beyond the work of art, we *are* the masterpiece.

May 1995

I Appeared to the Madonna

Vie d'(H)eros(es)

AUTOBIOGRAPHY

Either I am mistaken, or it is rare these days to find a man whose praises are sung by the masses, but who has not been the first to sing his own praise. There is so much egotism, and so great is the envy and hatred men feel for one another, that to make a name for yourself, it is not enough to do laudable things. You must either sing your own praise, or find someone in your stead who will constantly do it for you — which amounts to the same thing — by declaiming and loudly singing your praises to the masses so that others will be compelled, both by means of example and through their passion and perseverance, to repeat some of those praises. People are unlikely to rally around you of their own accord based on your great merits or on the worth of your great works. They will look on & remain eternally silent. If they can, they will prevent others from seeing these things. He who wishes to rise to great heights, even if his intent arises from genuine excellence, must forgo modesty. In this respect, too, the world is like women: you will never get anywhere with them through modesty & discretion.

— Leopardi, *Pensieri*, XXIV

END OF THE FIRST ACT

There is a nostalgia for things that never had a beginning.

To plant our own roots — not necessarily in terms of our birth — in the land of Otranto is to destine ourselves to a real-imaginary. It is precisely there, on the first day of one September, that I was born. Otranto. Always magnificent, a most religious bordello, a center of culture and of tolerance to bring together Islamic, Jewish, Turkish, and Catholic confluences. Its splendid cathedral, along with its magnificent mosaic that dates back to the year 1100 and that figures the "tree of life," serves as its witness.

A tolerance of such disparate currents, like the changing colors of the Ionian Sea, has never occurred in any other part of Italy. When referring to Puglia, we should never mistake it for that slice of Salento, also known as Magna Grecia, that extends further and further south until it reaches Capo Leuca. Where, until only a few years ago, the Greek dockworkers could be heard speaking in local dialects from Calimera, Gallipolli, etc.

So, to write an autobiography, however concise, based on our own not being there, on abandonment, on lack, and therefore drawing from the imaginary of this very same reality, means that Otranto was visited by a history that, including the invasion of the Turks, was and continues to be the cult (culture) of all the other histories excluded by this historical event.

Otranto. The cradle of excluded histories. Overseas mourning.

So, our failure to tell the story is not by chance, because it goes beyond chance. We find ourselves immersed in something that never had a beginning: an ethnicity married to an imaginary life. To be invented. For an extremely risky autobiography, both real and imaginary at the same time. Therefore, it is only thanks to this ethnic mayhem that the reader can continue to follow me.

Our peninsula never produced anything noteworthy in terms of Thought, if not, strangely enough, in the South. Here, we find the names of Giordano Bruno, Giambattista Vico, Tommaso Campanella, Croce, Gentile, etc., and the same Italian language that we inherited from Cielo and Federico II.

So, where this Thought *unthinks* itself, it becomes carefree, as it makes its way gradually further and further south until it reaches Capo Leuca. There where Magna Grecia begins. In the south of the South. Magna Grecia is the unthinking of the South's thought.

It is the South in decline. Its advantage. Despite being humiliated, insulted, vilified by deplorable consumerist oversaturation, it is still here.

It was here in the south of the South that the greatest saint among saints was born, he who exceeded the saintliness of sainthood: Giuseppe Desa da Copertino.

The only thing that remains for this crippled South is to fly.

Here we have the saint of flights — the *Holy of Holies'* supreme splendor: to levitate. Here we have "Frate Asino." Next to so much erudite interdisciplinarity. Grace is born not far from Copertino, the same year (1600) that they burn Thought in Campo de' Fiori (Giordano Bruno).

Ignorance is born. It's another fruit of Greek *mania*. The saint who has no sense of gravity is born. He levitates, he flies. People called him "Frate Asino," "he went around the world with his mouth hanging open." "Illiterate *&* a halfwit," he is the apotheosis of unthinking.

So, together, these real and imaginary origins are fundamental for what will follow with respect to my not being there. Inasmuch as they themselves rest on the void, so tolerant was Otranto's splendid church.

If not (dis)-graced by this privilege, there where misery is a luxury — or at least it was until recently — if not graced by such an ethnic premise, I would not have been able to access *being groundless*, to carefreeness, to an art that makes itself theater and that stages *the suspension of the tragic* after Nietzsche, the *unrepre-*

sentability, the *reaction shot* as *speaking*, *femininity* as *abandonment*, the end of the conflicted little theater of the "*I*" and its reprisals, the *lack* of what it consists.

I will attempt to daydream about the *feminine* as a chapter apart from *heroism*. So, there is a *heroism* of stage praxis that is the exact opposite of "heroic narration," therefore of identification and of performance, etc. And with respect to the "feminine," another fundamental chapter will be the one on "dongiovannism" & ostentatious "dongiovannism" as masochistic praxis of the presence of woman as interference.

Pater's *Imaginary Portraits* or Schwob's *Imaginary Lives* cannot be considered as intricate, eccentric exercises. In the very moment of its telling, every story is imaginary.

We'll laugh at our stories as if they were about other people, and our complicity is none other than a paradox invoked to bear witness to those events, which are extraneous to us.

It will reinforce the wavering certainty that those events ever happened.

On a road about 50 kilometers from Otranto, in Campi Salentina, an immense rural valley of grain, wine, grapes, and tobacco, especially tobacco, an Atlas of tobacco, is where my birth as Sardanapolus took place.

I see mountains of women "of all shapes," "of all ages" (we can estimate the actual number of female tobacco workers to be at least 1400). I find myself at four years old being passed around in the changing room of the plant by this mountain of womanly, animal nakedness, between breaks, assigned to either the sorting or to the various stages of processing and packaging the tobacco.

Beyond this, three religious orders: Piarists, Salesians, and Jesuits. Also, ancient Greek *&* Latin, speaking about anything and everything, ecclesiastical Latin, sports of course, every Saturday and Sunday. The reward: Lecce. Lecce as both reward and punishment.

From the time I was around three or four years old, I would serve at mass three or four times a day. I found my desire to celebrate the red while wearing the white altar dress fulfilled on feast days. So, an undeniable fascination with ritual, with the host, which I devoured with hunger — this eating the deconsecrated God — daily, because I had to get to school. While the others would come from home, I was there from six o'clock in the morning, having returned from the altars where, at first light, I had caressed my splendid blond Madonnas; they were as blond as the blondest Ceres, a little pagan, executed centuries ago by those extraordinary papier-mâché artisans from Lecce. Hence these blues, these silvers, these reds and golds, these pinks, these incenses.

From this paradise, from this wonderment, because childhood is wonderment when the misfortune of being born in the city does not befall us — childhood as the dark cellar's fright, fear sought after at any price, that same fear of which woman is made and which woman spurns by disallowing herself any abandon — from these, my extraordinary Madonnas, at the very moment that should have been my bliss, when I had returned to that mountain of tobacco which awaited me and which was my home, I would find myself in one of Dante's circles of hell, in an interference that I couldn't wait to cease so that I could return to my other life, which was marvelous, religious, non-existent.

This interference was comprised of naked women who would put on a particular kind of overalls up to their pubic region and slosh around in the muck, in an indescribable quantity of tobacco. The girls, 100, 200, 300 of them, would have a great deal of fun catching huge mice and tearing them apart with their teeth, or they would throw them at one another: this was their favorite game (and a game that, even now, I find suited to healthy young country girls, and to women that unkind nature has destined to remain eternally lacking in femininity).

Back in the church. Speaking Latin, responding in warped Latin, there too, myriads of women, the choir, boy sopranos. This ritual would later nauseate me. Even at the time, I found it offensive to piety.

The ritual as an outrage to an absent God would later destine me to that theatrical "Copernican revolution," to the "suspension of the tragic," to the refusal to be in history, in any history whatsoever, even and above all on the stage.

Refusing to grow up, like Pinocchio, is, if you will, the lock and key of my dismay tossed to the bottom of the sea. In the end, liberating me even from myself.

The refusal to grow up is the *conditio sine qua non* to the education of our "feminine." It is to refuse History and the conflict of the quotidian *historiette*.

We might title, to the *feminine* and to the refusal of History, two fundamental chapters of a life that I see myself leading as an obstinate, nonsensical "heroism." The descent to the battlefield, to the stage, seeking (through the reaction shot as speaking) all the histories excluded from that one history that occurred *&* from which we exclude ourselves, well even this is *heroic*.

Like Giuseppe Desa da Copertino, who, after half a lifetime of insistent requests that his favorite painting of the Madonna be sent to him in Osimo, suddenly realized the temptation that such an image would arouse in him, and he no longer wanted it. He glimpsed in that painting the terranean woman, subterranean, and he buried her within himself. I, too, forgot those marvelous Madonnas of mine, among whom I had taken shelter to ward off woman, and to whom I had masochistically delegated my superego. I took back from those Venuses the Madonna that I was in the name of pure absence.

And as a good, iconoclastic seven-year-old, I buried womanly saintliness deep down within myself. This was my first crusade against images. I found myself feeling like the Madonna at seven years old. And to feel like the Madonna at seven years old…

Having escaped this universe, I re-awoke to find myself attending law school, a 17-year-old at the University of Rome. I neglected my studies to dedicate myself to training for the theater. I understood immediately that I would need to prove myself, that I would need a debut, also because no one was going to give me a penny to get by in Rome as an actor, and, in this way, I was condemned to a premature debut.

So, it was Camus's *Caligula*. I debuted at 22, the head of a theater troupe and playing the lead role, whereas Alberto Ruggiero, whom I haven't seen since then, happened to be in charge of the direction.

It was a "triumph," both with the public and with the critics, in the sense that even though they tore the play apart, most of them recognized the birth of a "new" actor. My family convinced themselves that my life could not be anything but that: head of a theater troupe, administrator, translator, director, set designer, costume designer, leading actor. It had always already been written that I would take the stage only for "my debut."

Caligula marked the first decisive encounter of my life. Albert Camus. Venice. Teatro La Fenice. Outside-daytime. An encounter in three acts. My director friend and I were presenting a production to Camus (in '59 it was impossible for anyone to undertake a production of *Caligula*, since the author had suspended the rights, embittered, in his own words, by the terrible productions, of which the most abominable was the Piccolo Teatro di Milano's version with Renzo Ricci as the protagonist and Strehler, an exceptionally unfortunate actor, in the role of Scipione).

Camus listened attentively, and when he was finally persuaded, he asked very graciously who would play the leading role. "Me. Is that good enough for you?" "Three orange sodas," Camus said, smiling, to the waiter. The last three orange sodas, thank God; since we had gone so far as to say that we didn't drink to add a little spice to our good intentions for this momentous occasion, we were on our 30th most-blessed orange soda.

I had prepared for this debut with an extremely accelerated course, seven or eight hours a day, on fencing (*épée*, foil *&* saber) both at the academy and outside it as well, under the mentorship of Maestro Ammanato, along with a half-hour of boxing a day, a course that, due to my inexperience, would result in real matches with disastrous KOs. So, I dropped it almost immediately. I quit the academy as well... Yes, the academy: the only trace Pelosini had left was his name above the door to the poetic elocution room...

From then on, I studied poetic verse on my own, in private, with a portable Geloso tape recorder. And I kept it inside myself, just like last year, when I recited a raving Lectura Dantis, from the Torre degli Asinelli in Bologna in front of more than 100,000 people, for myself alone. All of it inside myself. Perhaps this was why so many people in the crowd were moved by it.

From the moment I arrived in Rome, I was the most talked-about person in the local police stations. Police chiefs *&* cops still remember my nocturnal sojourns in Piazza Euclide, Via Gotico, Piazza del Collegio Romano, San Vitale.

I would attract the attention of law enforcement officers by going around drunk in a tux and choking the necks of empty bottles: "A horse, a horse! My kingdom for a horse!"

In this way, I had the opportunity to find nocturnal friends and checkers partners — rather unfortunate partners, because I had learned the game well and at an advanced level from occasional customers at bars who took vacations, much longer than my own, in jail — in the all too obliging cops on duty whom I beat regularly, and who sometimes even lost more than a little money to me.

Brawls. Public order. Brawls. Not that I fought. I would instigate these brawls *&* then, having snuck away, delight in watching them.

Genoa. Not Campana's superb "Orphic" Genoa, but because I was broke after a grotesque wedding in Florence. A splendid villa in Sant'Ilario. A terrace that embraced the entire gulf, from Portofino to Sestri. A second run of *Caligula*, this time entirely under my direction at the Genoese Politeama, with Antonio Salines in the role of Scipione. Giancarlo Bignardi had even hand-painted the costumes for the occasion — the paint didn't dry until closing night — *&* Giannino Galloni proclaimed it a miracle in *L'Unità*: "... here is an actor, and we cannot say this strongly enough, who is new, full of ideas *&* technical abilities, to the point of excess."

Galloni, aside from being an extremely astute critic (the preceding quote not withstanding), was later the true founder of the Stabile di Genova theater. He had had the unfortunate idea to stage *Celestina*, judged scandalous at the time, for the inauguration, which made it necessary for him to resign.

At the Borsa di Arlecchino, by then the kingdom of Trionfo — a truly exceptional thespian, who was never given enough recognition by our rags — and at the Teatro Duse, almost simultaneously, I appeared in a version of *Doctor Jekyll* and in a production of *Tre atti unici* by an extraordinary madman called Marcello Barlocco.

So, to go from the abandonment of the natal agrarian village to the capital, from the mouse mountain that goes to Mohammed, Joyce's *Ulysses* was needed to have before me a language that gave the feeling of divine grace, unmediated by thought: *Ulysses* and *Finnegans Wake*.

So, there I was in Genoa, in this luxurious villa, where the rent went unpaid. There was very little money, and we had all abandoned ourselves to alcohol (the cost of the alcohol was figured in every performance), to cigarettes and all the rest, to the truly rather meager stagings, meager and luxurious at the same time.

Imagining a cosmos from this aorgic, Orphic folly began in Genoa. Certain ideas began to take shape and, more importantly, a praxis.

The unexpected. I discovered I was a father. I was on stage at the time and had a breakdown. "But that's impossible." "Come on, come and see the baby… Why won't you at least come and see the baby?" "But the baby is right here!" "What do you mean, is there another one?… What are you saying! It's your son!" "But I am my son."

I couldn't afford the luxury of being a father, the kind of paternity that only the false scholar and the Church can boast of. I wasn't capable. I needed to look after myself. "Here I am an orphan, what son."

I only went to see him many days later. "Don't you like him?" "No!" Indeed, I looked at myself in the mirror and didn't like what I saw. I never resigned myself to being a father. Thereafter, a loss would deprive me of the son of my son. He was five when he died. The stars held his destiny. Destiny knew all about my destitute circumstances to be both a son and a father, about the incompatibility, about my anxiety; it thus deprived me of the ambiguity of a reality.

Let's turn for a moment to women. It was precisely in Genoa that my Calvary as a Don Giovanni began. From then on, the *absence* of the Madonna that was in me, and which by then constituted my being, brought about the whole, far too obsessive praxis of the presence of women in my life and on the stage.

To be Don Giovanni to mortify the constant presence of a woman's body, of many women's bodies.

I never, or almost never, allowed there to be only one, and then only because I was distracted. We were always *many women*. Perhaps this is because you perpetually delude yourself into thinking that by putting several of them together, you can take the right eye from one, the left eye from another, an ear, the hair: it's a *mix* that you blend from two or three bodies to obtain that *desired* ash. The same with the legs, the breasts, etc.

The obsessive visitation of female bodies thus began in the name of the *Absence* safeguarded in me.

Don Giovanni is certainly not impotence — as certain foolish veins of feminism would have it. It is the *feminine* itself that verifies its own empty spaces in the mortification of the womanly body.

This collision with woman plays on the "impossibility," where discourse is only made possible inasmuch as it is conveyed by the "fashion industry" — lace, lace trim, underwear, bras, certain intimate garments (to be clear, it has nothing to do with fetishism).

It is here that the "naming," the undressing, starts; the rapport with the *feminine* is all there. So then, when we say "dongiovannism," we mean the *feminine*.

Here is where a *heroic* phase truly begins. Extremely noteworthy from the point of view of the reception, of the performance, of the distaste for all that is feminine which women lack.

In these my innocent Sardanapolian orgies, I saw a Michelangelian Sistina turned on its head, where the bodies are all clearly male and muscular. Most of all, I saw the odious identity that flourished even in young girls in flower, to the detriment of the *feminine*, in which they will no longer lose themselves, that will no longer characterize them.

I never met a woman who had so much as an ounce of the *feminine* in her.

Departing on a train that will never reach its destination — because we always depart by choosing our destination carefully — but we don't choose anything at all. No place. No arrival station.

So, as Don Giovanni, I didn't have a list of women in my head. I was full of *heroism*! And in the fullness of heroism, the "feminine" was entirely in the not-being there on my battlefields.

Abitare la battaglia [*The Story of Giuseppe Verdi*] — an extraordinary title from that exquisite person who was Gabriele Baldini — is likely the best book ever written on Verdi's melodramas, precisely because it was not written by an expert in the field, but rather by an Anglicist with a great passion for music.

It is a title that Sandro D'Amico still finds troubling.

Abitare la battaglia. Some works by Verdi are exactly that: this having inhabited the battle, the battle as *habitat*. All of Verdi's battles are from *Legnano*, in music, yes, but of a *domestic* nature. Everything that is romantically grandiose, patriotic, everything that inflames the passions, in these *feuilletons* that comprise the fullness of Verdi's music, in reality, takes place within the walls of the home. *Abitare la battaglia* is the expression that best suits me.

Of course, none of this suggests any rancor toward woman or women; if anything it suggests an infinite agape, in Schopenhauer's sense, if anything the infinite wonder that woman might not be *abandonment*. Look at the case of Ophelia in our *Hamlet*, a pupil of her own apprenticeship, in search of a masculine identity, since all identities are masculine, in her "haphazard rummaging" in the library of the Other: a perilous Alessandria of infinite reflections.

Women use these books as their mirror, and they only experience that moment of *unthinking* when before the mirror, in their ruinous *makeup*, because it is their *makeup* that destroys them, that annihilates them. This lesson on *makeup*, in which women destroy themselves, applies to the theater as well.

It's an extremely important lesson for theater.

Any woman who is speaking about a loss, or about Martin Heidegger, or about Lacan — because women are always ready to talk about anything and everything — will take something from her *makeup bag*, lipstick, some powder, and like an ape, even when speaking about her mother's recent death, will say: "She was such a good woman…" between one little stroke and another of the powder puff on her cheek. And in this cloud of powder, in this white dust, the Madonna vanishes. The divine on earth is lost.

Thus turning to all my wives, to all my harems, which I constantly changed, changed, changed, because the list is clearly something that comes later in the form of awareness, at the time it was only the imprecise form of a rose, petals on petals, blood stains and rose petals, without knowing exactly, in a Wildean fashion, which ones were the stains and which ones the rose petals, menses, hemorrhages and Tristans, female Tristans... Isoldes never encountered... It was a sum of Tristans. What emerged was the unfortunate Christ, a Wagnerian crucifixion turned on its head, without any women on the cross, for God's sake! A woman on the cross — Nietzsche reproached Wagner for that very thing — would be a dream!

There is always someone who is not there on the cross. A God is on the cross, not a woman.

On the cross of defamation there is the ego, the same. Defamation that effaces the ego, or at least it affronts it by calling it fastidious, arrogant, criminal, imbecilic. But not that sort of unthinking imbecility that is so yearned for, that sort of stupidity that sleeps with its mouth open, like the "idiot who would have liked to watch himself sleeping." This is the sin of never looking at ourselves enough as *idiots*.

This grace, this carefreeness that ought to attribute *a feminine* to woman, does not exist, and so someone will need to assume not only femininity, but also the idiocy of femininity, the *unthinking*.

Now, if you confront the theater question with these innate qualities, you realize that there is nothing more to ask, that there is nothing more to affirm or deny. You realize that the stage is an ideal floor of *emptiness*, the ring of *nothingness*, where we force open doors and Klossowski's breaths from his *Prince of Modifications* circulate, come and go. Klossowskian breath, from the Latin *flatus*. Breathing is this breath of the "Knights Templar's heroism" that continues to celebrate the anniversary of their own human bonfire in the eternal return (of eternity).

They'll make him a saint. My friend Pierre.

Klossowski and I share something very secret. I would say it is our secret that binds us. Klossowski promised himself that he would not die before seeing me recite his *Baphomet*. That flatters me. I will say that spending an evening, or a whole night, eating, drinking (even in this respect he exaggerates toward excess), and talking about God with Klossowski is a singular joy. Whenever we attend a banquet together, the guest, the honored guest, the one that secretly attracts us, is always somewhere else. It is by speaking to that person that we understand each other. Even when I start talking about sports. I always say the same things. I always repeat myself. When I talk about Brazilian soccer and of its other-worldly delights,

I say that "it plays elsewhere," and that the best commentary on it would come from ballet (?) critics, just like Clay's or Sugar Ray Leonard's boxing would need to have commentary from musical critics — as if "musical" critics actually existed. When I mention Borg, it is to refer to a certain frightening kind of concentration that would merit anything other than common discourse in tennis jargon. I always notice in these super (human) phenomena that which exceeds the human and renders them *admirable* beyond their sport, in which they are seemingly by chance, and therefore, in absolute perfection.

Since chance is always the absurd Kafkaian imperative that a nonsensical *heroism* accepts.

This is the legend, the myth.

This is why there cannot be a "great actor" unless we say "Great" without the actor, beyond the actor.

Stability, thy name is *drama*.

From Genoa to Rome. 1961. I needed a method. I needed to experiment a little, but not out in the open, not like people do today.

That was how the Teatro Laboratorio was born, where whoever wanted to could come whenever they wanted, and they could even watch the rehearsals. Moravia, Pasolini, Sandro Penna, Ennio Flaiano, Angelo Maria Ripellino, Elsa Morante, and many others would come to see me.

The Teatro Laboratorio began with *Hamlet* and, strangely enough, with *Pinocchio*, so Marlowe, etc.

When talking about me, people often refer erroneously to "basement theaters." No one knows why. My plays at that time were performed in traditional theaters, like the Arlecchino (now Teatro Flaiano), or Conte Partanna's Teatro dei Satiri, or the Teatro delle Arti.

I only worked in a basement theater twice, in 1967 no less; that is, before I left the theater after an unforgettable revival of *Salome*.

There also seems to be a good deal of misunderstanding about my literary incursions during that period.

In reality, it was a study of *musicality* in the form of writing. It arose from listening to music, more than anything else, though never searching for anything specifically musical, rejecting Bona's method, and, therefore, any approach in the name of eighth notes or sixteenth notes, etc.

Completely off the staff. Like Di Stefano, whom I met two years ago, and whose voice I have always considered the most beautiful voice ever heard.

Milan was an occasion for our shared merrymaking. We're still the greatest of friends to this day, and he often amuses himself by saying, "I am the Carmelo Bene of music. Ah music! I never knew how to read music, and I never want to learn."

This from the young man who, barely 22 years old, was defined by Toscanini as "the most beautiful voice of all time."

"All the others are tenors," he said. What I have always gone around saying, "All the others are actors."

So, it wasn't so much looking for an interdisciplinary methodology, but rather, in my literary praxis, for a musicality even in writing. Harboring the antihumanistic necessity par excellence. Harboring "lady" *indiscipline*.

I referred, precisely in *Italian Credit V.E.R.D.I.*, to a "me" that in all likelihood never existed: "If the world were how we see it and not how the world sees us, perhaps we would be more discreet." If they had figured out, at the very least, these nuances, then they would have figured out the reason for a scandal. But more importantly, they would have understood that, even at the beginning, it was always about the *scandal of reason*. Instead, they made it the reason for scandal.

Unprepared as ever, crammed like a bunch of Laforguian baubles on the *étagère* of genres.

Even if it was immature at the beginning, my (genre) *degeneracy* could not find an audience. It still cannot find one to this day. Precisely because it is *degeneration* and therefore the *de-stabilization* of any and every "genre."

It could be said that I had already amassed a great deal of theater experience because of faith, and that I, therefore, never needed to practice. My praxis also never had a beginning. It began in a fourth movement, a fifth, a sixth, who knows where... Who knows where it began.

To tell the truth, my theater began precisely when I finished out my sentence, where there was nothing to say, but to be said.

When I realized that I was ready to devote myself to another cult, a more profound religion, I was able to do so because I was ready to dedicate myself to something *other*.

The Teatro Laboratorio in Trastevere, number 23 in Piazza San Cosimato, in a courtyard that resembles the prison at Sing Sing, all covered in iron grating, grills, a famous seven-, or eight-story building.

Very young and head of a theater company, without a penny to my name, surrounded by extraordinary zany actors found in Borgo Santo Spirito by Signora d'Origlia and the knight Palmi, my very good friends.

I often visited that place, pleasantly full of clamorous theatricality, where later stolid, uncultured, Roman pseudo-intellectuals would come to deride those stories of saints, of carts, of Shakespeare distorted in exaltation, of Hamlets that started in Elsinore and ended in Cascia...

It was there. That is where I found wonderment in its entirety. And with me, maybe only Arbasino who cited the theater & myself in *Grazie per le magnifiche rose*, the best example of Italian theater of the second half of the 20th century; that honors me.

That was our incubator. Some aging zany actors, the Nistris, the Allegrinis, some young blood as well, Luigi Mezzanotte, who was 17 at the time, & Alfiero Vincenti, "the martyr of Otranto."

Extraordinary things: Signorina Palmi who would turn the lights on and off: "No, not that one! It's this one!" "A red one!" "No, here we need a green one!" "Signorina, you're mistaken." All with the audience in the theater.

Magnificent, divine amnesias, continuous voids of stages made-up from unreliable pauses. These "ghosts" of Hamlet's father who would exit the stage in Manlio Nevastri's (stage name Nastri) corpulent body, dragging along the tower's merlons in the "farewell." This knight was preaching to the fish on a board representing the sea — but they had forgotten to nail it to the exterior — that was swinging back & forth, and kept moving the script he was meant to read with his back to the audience. Such that the knight, too, was bouncing back and forth all over the small stage, all the while weeping and beseeching, "Stop the sea, stop the sea!"

There was a constant confusion of identities, between Allegrini, Nistri, & Palmi, since in that theater they performed four or five plays a day, so that "Good day Count!" "No, what do you mean Count?" "I'm the Prince, he can't be the Count!"

They split up the parts in this way, in front of an audience that was trying to understand what was going on, and thinking they were speaking softly — but by this point all of them were deaf — they were shouting questions at one another. "No, wait a minute," the knight would say. "What's going on, who are you?" "I'm the Duke, Knight, the Duke!" "...Wait a minute, wait a minute, wait a minute..." And they kept on characterizing themselves endlessly, indifferent to the amused audience that was pissing its pants, "wait a minute, wait a minute, wait a minute... because... if he's the Duke, and you're the Count... then... who am I?"

Simply divine.

These were extraordinary derisions on the identico's loss, which was thus minimized by the pantographs of the void of memory.

Other times, the Knight, filled with fervor, rushed onto the stage and attacked with force, just like an implacable boxer who means to end the match before the bell, with skull in hand: "To be or not to be..." — dissuaded by loud voices from the wings.

Dazed from the chatter, distracted, he would get stuck only to start again with even more dogged determination: "to die, to sleep, nothing…" And the same cherubs who took it upon themselves to silence him, now on stage, were binding him ever so gently, ever so humanely, in a straitjacket to lead him off stage, to the reality of the intermission. Was it possible that the Knight was crazy? Not at all, it was simply that the curtain hadn't been drawn. The Knight hadn't noticed, that's all.

Just like how he never noticed those pages torn from his script, copied and pasted in the pages of a newspaper, in the most unscrupulous comedies. But the audience certainly noticed, because a fainthearted light, backlit, mercilessly decried this and other similar flaws of that involuntary hero who was Bruno Emanuel Palmi.

That habitual, stooped-over fighting of his, day after day, with his rival, the prompter, who was swallowed up far below in the bottom of the pit under a Michelangelian cupola, almost to challenge tangentially the proscenium above: "Speak, coward, Speak to me!… You were granted the gift of speech, why do you not speak?!" A creator infuriated by his little Moses who was not speaking, it's true, but who was screaming from the bottom of his centennial duty: creature and creator, unrestrained involuntary accomplices, at the mercy of defeating grace.

No imbecilic garmented apparition was ever lurking in that truly unrepresentable theater.

Checkmate to the role, considering that those same young people found themselves somehow catapulted onto that stage of sovereign amnesia, void of cues and directions.

On another occasion, Luigi Mezzanotte, playing his first part as a condemned man — in a performance of *Caterina da Siena*, I don't recall which one — was chained to the base of the gallows with a very long chain, where he endured a rather lengthy sermon and its eventual confession wrested from him by Saint Caterina Signorina Annamaria Palmi, who was extraordinarily overtaken by her love of God.

Once he had been executed, and the curtain had fallen, it seemed natural to poor Gigi (who thought at the beginning, like everyone else, that the theater was a fiction) that he would be liberated from the infamous chain that had been fastened to his wrists with an enormous rusty lock — three turns of an infernal key and off he would go.

Well, it was the key that had gone off somewhere. And who knew where. Yes, where had it gone? It was getting late. Late for the impatient guardian and late for the victim who had naively planned to go home after the performance. In short, Gigi slept in the theater, chained to his role, until the following morning, when

Vulcan, from across the street, appeared & liberated him from his nightmare.

Genoveffa di Brabante, *La Nemica*, *Romeo and Juliet*, *Pia de' Tolomei*, so many wonderful occasions to disaffirm...

During their tours of asylums, one of the actors would invariably get lost, only to turn up two or three days later in a straitjacket by "mistake."

It's true. This heaven-sent, award-winning theater company found its most attentive and numerous audiences among the insane. Even I, myself, once awoke to find myself in the insane asylum. It was the day after I had told my father about my foolish plan to get married when I was 20 (anyone who intends to share "a life" with terrestrial woman ought to be arrested immediately and placed under psychiatric care). I was righteously evangelizing in the courtyard — a long crimson satin dressing gown earned me the right to be called by the name of Mohammed among those religious people from elsewhere. 10 days. And what performances they were! I'll never have an audience like that again. Extraordinary & moved. No joke... Under a torrential rain, almost purposefully precipitous to dampen the torture of "Un bel dì vedremo" playing on the radio, a carriage-taxi out of a novel, with my betrothed enemy inside, tore me away from that theater where I still hope to return.

For now, let's stick to the matter at hand: the knight Palmi in *Romeo and Juliet*, a painted octogenarian with bright red cheeks, his face covered in powder like a fragile fresco, and wearing skeletal black-violet tights, is more in love than ever as he leans heavily against a papered wall that breaks, revealing Signorina Annamaria on a wobbly stool — "Why are you Romeo?"— the same stool that she used as a cloud in more saintly performances while, indomitable, throwing bunches of flowers in the air & yelling in a marked Romagnol accent in the catharsis of "apotheosis."

O Amnesia of loves! It was love undone by amnesia.

Signora D'Origlia, utterly incapable of telling lies on stage, allowed herself to tell a wicked little lie every now and then in her life; like that stunt she pulled at customs on her way back from Lourdes. There was only one stain in the otherwise innocent trunk of the car. Two or three bottles of anisette that required explanation: "Some holy water, just some holy water!" was the lie Signora Bianca told. An unprincipled atheist, the customs official uncorked a bottle & sniffed, "This is anisette!"

"Anisette?!" The signora was shocked. That is until divine Grace removed every obstacle from her path. Throwing her arms around her husband and crying real tears, she began shouting, "Bruno, Bruno, did you hear that? It isn't water! It's a miracle, a miracle!..."

In the end, we're always on stage, where we would find Signora Bianca, alone with the audience, always waiting half hours for her consort to arrive. Whenever this happened, she would play for time: "Eh, I see him, I see him, he's pretty far away, maybe a kilometer... he's getting closer... now I can see him more clearly... Oh God, he's stumbling, he's falling, he's getting up again..." etc.

If Christ had happened to find himself among those zany actors his Calvary would have been endless. He would undoubtedly still be up there, forgotten on the cross, babbling like an idiot about his increasingly miserable agony.

Already a pluri-octogenarian, the half-naked knight Palmi was lifted with all his wrinkles onto a cross that was outrageous enough to provoke that unfortunate man's rage on a stage-altar studded with lights from a cheap amusement park, and on Good Friday evening to boot ("in Santo Spirito" would be an apt phrase).

In the name of God, duly absent, the old man agonized willingly with the infinite patience of a martyr who was waiting only for the pious-Madonna-at-his-feet to exhale a farewell to that "last (supper) scene."

That mystic fool, hanging there & murmuring, his strength spent & incapable of enduring it any longer, suffered as anguished an agony as ever there was one.

To betray the script that time, a wicked centurion disguised as an authors' rights agent from the SIAE was holding up Madame D'Origlia, by the hem of her Madonna costume, and demanding that day's remittance slip.

"Give it to me!" the villain said, losing his patience. "Can't we do it after Christ's agony…" the holy mother pleaded with legitimate concern. "Forgive me, Signora, but what agony are you talking about… I don't have time for agonies…" "But look, you understand, that poor man is hanging on a cross… he's been waiting to die for over an hour… let him die and then we'll take care of the remittance slip." "All right, let him die, let him die… He'd better get on with it!" "Never you mind. I'll make him die in no time."

So the Madonna took the stage and laid it on thick for that suffering Christ with a chain of "o"s: "Oooooo… Bruno!… Bruno!… where did you put the remittance slip?" all the while at the foot of this immense cross that was no longer standing, because it, too, was weary of waiting. "In the first drawer of the chest of drawers, where we keep the false eyelashes… in your dressing room…" And he finally took his last breath, much to the delight of the Authors' Rights Society.

I have never seen another theater like it, of such greatness, even if it was involuntary. Everything else is the contemptible professionalism of laborer-actors always ready to say their lines.

When faced with the merciless moments of amnesia that would unexpectedly overtake the knight Palmi, the only thing he could do was fall to his knees. In order to escape from the bottomless voids into which the knight would fall while on stage, and which became more frequent with age, in his last years, he would fill that void with a peremptory off-script "Farewell!..." He would throw reason aside and suddenly utter the felicitous "Farewell!... Farewell!"

Even in the same play, a sequence of amnesiac moments would resolve themselves in a series of "Farewells!" — from melancholy to melodramatic, in accordance with the occasion, in every sort of tone.

Farewell theater, farewell lies, farewell self, farewell all, farewell actor-performer and farewell identity, farewell for good.

My entire theater experience begins with the "farewell." First there is the farewell, and then the non-History, the non-event, which coincides with what occurs, until the stage sleeps. The farewell is a necessity that comes *prior* to the *premise*. Without the "farewell," there can be no beginning.

Alfiero Vincenti — who would later perform an amazing King in my film, stage, television, and radio versions of *Hamlet* — was Alessandro Serenelli in the drama *Beata Maria Goretti*. And who, if not the virgin Signorina Annamaria Palmi, could play that role in that backstreet theater packed with all those sweet nuns, small children, and cardinals.

In order to exalt the virgin Goretti's holiness, no tactic went untried: threats, the morbidly-brandished sickle, and the streams of obscene demonic insults "by subject" that were hurled at her: "slut, whore... I'll do this to you... I'll break your other one..." An overflowing of obscenities to accentuate the sainthood of Signorina Palmi, who felt very much at ease in her flagellated victim's attire. All this was tolerated in principle, because attributed to the vulgar Tempter, even though the cardinals were exchanging somewhat wild-eyed, skeptical glances.

In truth, it was outright vulgar, a bit like back in the 13th century when veritable orgies were permitted in churches to provide an example of the sins people should absolutely not commit.

Whispering winds and gales — many of which, as fate would have it, hailed from the same parentage as those from Borgo Santo Spirito — were circulating around the Teatro Laboratorio. After an invariably long wait — at times, as many as three hours — the audience members were obliged to present themselves to "make-up" in the adjacent entrance hall. Once there, Signor Nistri, who always wore an impeccable tuxedo and gaiters on his shoes (all stuff he found at Porta Portese) while preserving an heroic dignity, and I would disfigure *ad libitum* the faces of our "season ticket holders" who, during intermission, would first receive buckets of water dumped on their fake, snobbish voyeurism (wavering between "sons of bitches" and "... it's nice, this place, though rather peculiar...!") and then they would go to the bar next door, where they would see themselves in the mirror, made-up by hacks, so they couldn't criticize anything or tear apart the repertory of their values, because they had been derided by the make-up that effaced them.

We put make-up on them for this reason: so that it would be impossible to take seriously any of their judgments. We cut the ground from under their feet to neutralize any potential rumors. These stunts were healthy injections of pessimism that would end up with laughs before the mirror.

Of course, Alberto Greco was with me at that time. The great Argentinian painter who, by preaching "Arte-Vivo," presented his best tempera to the wonderful-random-outrage of knurled tires that cut through asphalt.

Dangerously inured to not drinking, it so happened that I found him sloshed on stage — on opening night, no less, of *Cristo '63*, in the role of John the Apostle, no less, and in a theater packed with an unlikely number of 120 Christians, all bent over *&* rubbing up against one another in clamorous promiscuity.

Perhaps compelled — what do I know... poor Christ in that case — by an urgent need, filled to the "brim," my dear Alberto allowed himself to moisten, with a shower of urine, the silhouettes of the Argentinian ambassador, his wife who was unfortunate enough to be sitting beside him, and the cultural attaché next to her in the front row.

Thus transformed into that other John (Giovanni Battista), new defamatory ideas came to him for the cakes from the "Last Supper" scene, which had been staged for the performance with a luxuriousness that was a tad excessive & certainly for a far more "saintly" occasion.

Having drained the source of the golden shower, the drunkard creatively flung, one after another, handfuls of whipped cream & liquor-infused dough at the three compatriots who were nailed to their seats in a stuporous, incredulous, dignified steadiness. They were refined by the viscous slime & dough that was getting thicker, like glue on their defamed pride.

By this point, that (genre) degenerate had translated into his habitual role as a paint-slinger; best to have his hand in a trowel and slather it on to refinish humans' outer appearances "to get it just right" (clothing, heads of hair, fur coats, etc.). So, from the whipped cream to all that remains: "Spagheti, passame!"

The other zany actors, his accomplices on stage, were drawn into that schizoid orgy of matter in unrestrained drive and passed around to that, by now insane, collective repugnant clumps of stringy spaghetti which the madman smeared on yielding heads that began to drip with a dreadful mixed ragout. The ambassador, in particular, looked like the statue of the Commendatore, petrified in the face of that torrential flow.

It was a truly unforgettable evening.

The *destruens* thrill, as is natural, spread rapidly through the 120, and the performance was wonderful. The Argentinian embassy was converted into a block of waste.

The ambassador himself enjoyed the play more than a little, since the next day he ardently requested that the theater be closed so that the performance would forever remain unrepeatable.

And unrepeatable it remained. A stunning anticipation of the *happenings* that would follow in the years to come.

The only miracle I could perform as Christ was to "turn off the light" on that unfortunate tableau. Uselessly. There were those who captured the affair, firing tempestuous flashes on that infamy.

Thank God for the photographs! They were the reason for my absolution, "for not having committed the act."

As it was, there were loads of idiots who enjoyed going around and writing concocted stories in which they claimed that I was the one who urinated all over Latin soil. Slander that crucified me up until just a few years ago.

The Teatro Laboratorio in Rome was closed for good. A summary trial. During the trial, they talked about a preventive arrest, since both the newspapers and the tabloids had printed front page stories about the profanation perpetrated by the Antichrist that everyone wanted to be me and not my favorite Argentinian apostle who hastily fled to Spain, perhaps to baptize other embassies and to preach "Arte-Vivo" to an audience, *naturaliter*, more accustomed to his idiom.

Well, I should stay out of sight for at least a month. That's what a lawyer, my patient among the most assiduous of the chosen ones from my ex-theater, told me. I laid low *&* meditated, moving my residence every three days, from villa to villa, from street to street, disguised as an Arab, cloaked like a Berber, to avoid calling attention to myself and also because those fortunate clothes — white and blue — were the only ones I had thanks to certain of my African friends, who were always happy devourers of sweets made with Kief. I wandered around like that, night after night, as if I'd either lost my mind or left a costume shop. I had never been less bothered by the police who, though tempted, happily left me alone to avoid committing a sulfurous troglodyte's sin.

I worked on several projects, transforming them in no time into official plays: Marlowe's *Edward II* (Teatro Arlecchino), Jarry's *Ubu Roi* (Teatro dei Satiri), and finally Oscar Wilde's now historic *Salome* (Teatro Delle Muse), which was greeted with ovation after ovation and whistles from an elite crowd — faithful supporters such as Ennio Flaiano, Arbasino, Moravia, and Francis Lane were there along with staunch haughty detractors.

Born from unthinking suffering — after a few hours of rehearsals with Franco Citti, an extraordinary "Baptist," and Alfredino Leggi, at the time both guests serving mandated sentences in Ceccano; and with Vincenti, who would later prove his worth as an actor in successive versions of *Hamlet* — played in the midst of incense, in secondhand red and gold costumes; the set represented a post-war of extinguished bottles, this *Salome* suddenly imposed itself on the universe of Roman provincialism and on penny-ante Italian critics.

"This wonderful *Salome*," Alberto Arbasino wrote, "had the merit to serve as irrefutable proof by thus setting apart the smart people from the duds."

We discover in its creator, *chez nous*, a "côté Artaud" (the Brechtian one, since at this point Strehler's production is predictable).

The *Borghese* magazine got carried away: "... There is nothing that theater critics can do in this case. It's a matter for the police!" Poor Flaiano. As a recidivist Simonist, he was banned for a time from any and all blessed cultural gatherings in the capital for having given an encore of a "piece" in the *Europeo* (*Il rosa et il nero*), sending Giuseppe Patroni Griffi back to school. John Francis Lane from the *Times* took issue with this same "author of *Il Mare*."

To the *"enfant terrible"* I had earned from the immaculate and silvery performance of the previous "Marlowe," we can now add (fatal springs of misunderstandings nevertheless running through "my theater") — also attributed to Flaiano — the "*desecration*," a stage voice coined for me alone, clearly in the sense of *demystifying*. Certainly not! It was useless to explain myself, to translate the words of that Ennio of ours. Certainly not! Nothing to be done about it. So now I am definitively Simon the Sorcerer, a profaner of altar-texts, and "Hell — the eternal heat *&* cold of complete idiocy, in charge and not of the works — No doubt about it."

24 years old. Misunderstandings everywhere *&*, even worse, growing, inversely proportional to my first and last names which were by this time appearing in the newspapers (always distorted up until then) in their incredible recorded mirage: melos-carme-mountain.

We might even call them "detective story" misunderstandings, in the manner of the ineffable "august" *historiette* from the brutal Scelba-Scarpia police. For example, one beautiful October afternoon, Rome was azure (at the time we were doing a repeat performance of *Ubu Roi* at the Teatro dei Satiri, thanks to the patronage of my friend Count Partanna, an anxious tenant who was in a bad way), when the theater was invaded by several police squads, some of the cops were guarding the entrances and exits, while the others — even more absurd — were searching the stage and backstage. They claimed they were looking for a "tableau of the Madonna."

While my attention was focused on contemplating I don't know which body, I was ordered by phone to make my chivalrous way, immediately, to "the scene of the crime." Ever sensitive to soldier's orders, I complied, and, once on the scene, the sweaty uniforms confessed that they were from the "vice squad" and had been inconvenienced by an anonymous complaint which required that they track down and then seize an unspecified object, indeed, an abhorrent image, either a sculpture or a painting, of Our Lady in an inappropriate & unbecoming manner.

So, they got to work searching the place determinedly, and not without damages to all those old odds and ends with which this occasion presented them in the dark. And what is truly insane (insane for anyone unfamiliar with the sworn blindness of the Amatrician Knights Templar), I say, endangering their own lives, since a halberd, abandoned by some inattentive medieval suit of armor clothed in dust, weary of all that useless clamoring, suddenly plunged its pike into the unfortunate investigator's skull.

The mercenary captain, in the process of hurting himself elsewhere, rushed toward the sound of whiskery cries resembling a mouse stuck in a tight spot, stumbling to ascertain the rather pitiful state that heaven had granted, thanks to the investigation's zeal and glory, to its hero in that Thermopylae (for everything was falling on the heroes' heads from the chaotic wardrobes in the blind vaults in the cellar). He attacked the theater's "Persian" guardian, shouting his head off at him, and disarmed him in a flash of his lamp, the only "weapon" that provided light in that darkness, and whose shattered light faded on the ungrateful earth. And then it was dark — O Simonides! — nothingness.

And gradually in that din of horrid pots and pans — who among those wretches would not have sought honorable resistance before succumbing? — a line of helmets on the shields taken away from those heroes in dead armor that were raised as if umbrellas against irreparable harm. Merciless Mars! Oh, if only all that cruel sacrifice would have, at the end of the battle, earned them the object that their iconoclastic fury had chosen to locate in order to burn! If only the "unnamed whisper" would have been a little less sibylline and had better described the "tableau," it would have spared those courageous men!...

Certainly not! A God-fearing spectator had, in fact, reported to the police a "tableau" of the Virgin Mary that didn't have an ounce of piety in it; on the contrary, it was rather offensive; but, good God!, he could have made it clear that when he said "tableau" he was referring to a "tableau" from the script, that is to say an irreverent scene from that notorious play, and not an actual object that, without existing, ended up causing so much slaughter and bloodshed.

ACTRESSES

I helped her wither,
Fate took care of the rest...

J. Laforgue

Hair bleached ash blond, toenails still bearing traces of red polish, posthumous leftovers from the makeup for that Pompeian fresco in which I enjoyed passing time with Herod Antipas, drunk and half dead, I was swaying back and forth in an Odyssean hammock in a lovely garden full of flowers, a guest of the sorceress Elsa de Giorgi in "her" Circeo.

The unfamiliar blond hair of a very beautiful, statuesque Roman girl with green eyes brushed against me. She was destined by the gods to be by my side from that moment for another 18 years.

I said to be by my side, which is the same as saying unimaginable and serene separation (at least in the early years), much to the dismay of the senseless — at this point exhausted — entangling of bodies.

I have said elsewhere — though I'm not certain where — that the embrace — each face facing the elsewhere of the eyes — is the most experienced misunderstanding of their respective images, that love debased by intercourse is like a person in the throes of death, who, horrified, sees what he is holding close to his chest slipping away from him in deep water (and, therefore, he holds it tightly), only content when he feels this urgency drown in that nothingness.

So, she was my favorite among the 100 from my then empty bed. Lydia shined from incomprehension with respect to her divine heights. More devoted to me than any other woman had ever been, she deluded herself into thinking that discourse — my discourse — might be something other than — my — discourse about life. "She stuck to the facts" ("nice" those facts, even in their etymology). Oh, if only she had listened, even for a moment! But what do you expect? Like every most saintly woman, she took the *saying*, the discourse, for the most wonderful opportunity in her life to *converse*. Like all women, she starved herself of the fundamental theological elements, everything about her was a "repeat performance." And she vanished. Little by little, like someone who withdraws from the stage in a capricious search for her own light, she found herself in the wings. Plain and simple.

God knows how useless it is to inject a single drop of femininity into a womanly creature. These women do possess severe manliness, an implacable hostility toward definitive abandonment. Inartistic "par excellence," these Amazons who are more ferocious, the more they are enamored Penthesileas, still today, continue to raise the socio-historical misunderstanding on the "woman question," and many fools bemoan the state of these "unfortunates," agreeing that woman has always been disfigured by male history; that this "woman," therefore, has within herself many surprise miracles, that it is only the arrogant politics of vulgar men that prohibits them from carrying them out — yes, my good fellows, from "expressing themselves."

Madness. Since the beginning & forever and ever after, that which has been designated as "art history" (without history) would have had an illicit affair with its step-sister history; yes, but always in its revealing itself as "feminine," indeed, like the swooning of history.

So, it is clear how the always inopportune, hoped for liberation of woman is above all a misconception of the aesthetic sphere.

"Woman" is *intended* to emancipate herself from the *feminine*, from *unthinking*, etc. The woman-"thing" demands its reappropriation, alas legalized, of the *masculine* that has always been *her own*, for God's sake.

And I saw Pinocchio and my own destiny.

In one pocket Hamlet & in the other Pinocchio — God only knows how much my kidneys and buttocks were worn out from the, by no means romantic, sleeping — from a summer of sleeping outdoors, oh, hell's bells! — A tempest destroyed a big top tent I had constructed *ad hoc* in the square, this, too, without beds, for the so-called two asses festival. The rain, undoubtedly blessed by the Court of Miracles, who are still the musical hosts in charge of that "international" place of gatherings — for me collisions with cobbled streets and quixotic tension with Aurora's rosy fingers — nothing remained of the circus-theater after so much rain from the tempest. We didn't think it "appropriate" to allow ourselves to take cover in the sacristies. And it ended there.

In that land that was once Franciscan and made inhospitable from the foolishness of an elite naturally disposed to the privilege of American yearnings, and to wage battle against the otherwise talented — yes, because impossible — homegrown fannies, I solidified my friendship with Roberto Lerici (who had, among his most recent "senseless overindulgences," published my first reworking of Collodi). My *débâcle* was made public, solar, and Roberto repaired it — excessive *fair play* in good faith — by inviting "the" Carmelo and a certain Lydia to either breakfast or lunch. The poor other zany actors were flood victims, half-dressed and inevitably on a diet, in attendance, though invisible beyond the hedges of those restaurant terraces: they smelled certain divine odors that the summer breeze permitted them from our altar-table laden with food. That's how it is.

Roberto and I planned to meet again in Versilia the following August, so that we might experiment with a text that I had in mind to compose entirely for myself.

Having declared eternal war against those obnoxious boors, everything fell apart, and I awoke elsewhere.

Back in Otranto. A guest of my parents, to whom I owe nearly everything that I was allowed to (un)do.

The immense, white Arab house, with one side facing the Sticchi's irrational Moorish villa, with its golden cupola that dominates the hot springs of Santa Cesarea, the cliffs and the Ionian Sea, a peacock of infinite enchanted waves. On clear days, you can pick out pink Albania from those arched balconies. At all times, you sense that, here, life has been willfully chosen. A sad, sad riddle fades on the sea bottom of black billows, painted again and again below that infinite azure. Azure Africa. Immediately below is the sulfurous rumbling — a mourning coffin among the gargantuan rocks, a hideous body that rips itself apart on them.

You need only raise your eyes a little and the water, another, very deep water, cradles the expanse with gold and silver, a tempestuous meadow of turquoise and emerald.

C+ on that essay, the first of my literary incursions. I wrote *Our Lady of the Turks*, a novel, for the publishing house Sugar in less than a month. From the very first page, I knew that I was spitting out a masterpiece. And it was, even if it was overlooked by certain hacks.

Our Lady... is not only "an amusing parody of interior life," a Des Esseintes deflated and ridiculed. No sir. It is definitely something else. It is the most beautiful piece, in the form of an historical novel, on my south of the South. Read it for yourself or tell those natives about it and see if they will not find it fits them perfectly, like a *fado* from their greatest bard. "Modesty": *jamais couché avec*.

With respect to the history of 20th-century Italian literature (I am either excluded or not tolerated, *deo gratias*), "it is better to remain silent." The volumes that chronicle the entire century mostly flaunt a rather beautiful and nonchalant Dannunzian absence. The period post-Hitler exhausts itself with recycling weighty and inane examinations of the great nothingness that is there. The Landolfis, the Flaianos, the Longanesis, alongside the Arbasinos are considered masters by few. Pasolini's best work is in *Salò-Sade*, that is, if we exclude the translator and philologist Pier Paolo, the best craftsman of his Friulian language. In this our provincial-cinematic-like, dis-emperored downfall, it was the common fate for those (three or four) who were "different" to sacrifice outside the "lines."

The ludicrous and carefree sloppiness in the time of the literary crisis was shocking beyond imagination; the only effort that was made was to shorten the "range," simplifying certain "outbursts" from the present — already the culture page is, in and of itself, so mortifying — thus the hostility between "spoken" and "written" is superseded by the writing of the masses, not at all intended for those extremely rare "born" writers who abstain from both reading and writing contemporary works. It all happened just as Giacomo Leopardi prophesized in 1820; that nowadays a writer's apex comes from scrambling up to a newspaper's headlines and — like in any local festival — once there, to sit down and write Salgarian stories with universal appeal of things like war and similar *bagatelles*.

And like that, (Ah! the accident) should a casual glance fall on a page from D'Annunzio, crucified on the *martyre* of his own mother tongue, oh, should that occur, it would be a relief. You always find in his entangled brambles, even between his death rattles, as unspoken as you like, the last *saying*. And then there was Tarchetti, Dossi, and Campana, Guido Gozzano, Gadda, the commissioner Pizzuto... And that's it.

ENTRACTE

Oh yeah: "Would you like a wonderful totalitarian injustice?"
                                                         C. Pavese

Or, if you prefer:

When he was a child, a monk had taught him that injustice and enemies do not exist. Since everything is a vast pine grove... Go to sleep, let's change the flowers... If I weren't a building, they might believe me.

                                                   Our Lady of the Turks

The solemn and admittedly humble lesson that the Paters, the William Morrises, the Millais, and the Rossettis inflicted upon themselves — ah alas — was *décadence*, as it should be intended: a reshaping of history and of "creative" art in general by way of an exasperated *critical sense*.

An extraordinary period where *criticism is art*, a bridge of flowers — soul, haywire — going back to the Italy of the 15th century. A time of dispositions & discontents, painted in the true sky, identical — in the failed wager to be won — only to that other one, unadorned, the inestimable era of the Antoninis.

Flowers, yes, but for skirts. Flowered skirts. Skirts with or without women. Either rugs or tiles, a design prefigured by Ingres in the obtrusive cellulite of his models, bodies forgotten like sponges on the multicolored motifs in bathrooms.

A time (mine) to bid farewell to Plutarch who doesn't understand Alexander the Great: all his infantile Greek language to amuse himself with war (war of "transition," of "dusk" — a praxis from *Zarathustra*, millennia earlier), enough to beat his head against a wall in China, *beyond the principle of victory*.

So, what does our good criminal Plutarch do? He compares him to a statist *&* military dictator, Cæsar, who, in his time, was seen crying from envy — or so they say — but I rather think it was from his incomprehension of the never-ending exploits *&* triumphs of that young man outside history, and, instead, determined to measure his precocious knowledge by the geographical irony of the journey.

For Plutarch, now an old child, all that remains is to spell out "parallel" summaries of this and that maneuver from those field strategists. His dangerous digressions ruined more than a few minds with respect to Giambattista Vico's refluxes about noble and ethical history: from Schiller to the most Verdian of librettos. Wherefore, a silence and then swastikas, sashes and lunacy and horror. Now, for example, it's not all that fashionable. But it will be tomorrow. It's already tomorrow.

It is, in and of itself, a crime to teach. If, furthermore, the "subject" is history, then it is a double crime, and if that history is the one that Gibbon champions, then the crime is increased to the third power. It's a recidivist apologia for slaughter.

Why not translate Herodian? What are we waiting for? He left us the only piece of writing in exquisite Greek that conveyed our venerable history. Herodian has been translated *&* circulated throughout the entire world, except in Italy. The entire world is aware of our history, except us, and it's not even all that old. We satisfy ourselves with rumors — as amusing as these can be — about Suetonius *&* Dion.

Mommsen *&* Gibbon, deafened by the thunder of cannon balls, desiccated humans with blind vampire eyes, with their dense cadaver's breath, continue to be taught in schools, glorifying the "magical" ostentation of *"creative" history*.

Art, ah alas, art, after the fresco, an elegantly sketched summer storm that was the grace of the Pre-Raphaelites, persisted in the delusional droughts of the eternal da capos. Then there's music, even music is *creative*. Theater after Nietzsche is *creative*. Our actor is annoyingly "present," without being or not being there: he is *creative* in his *genre*. The "critics" have returned to doze in the orchestra. On stage, we "think" and refer to things we've "thought about"; the "masculine" enrages women actresses (and actors). "O like everything it is a stupefying fair!" "Questionable," indeed.

Do you know what I do in the morning when I'm on the toilet and I allow myself to think? I think that "artist" and "woman" would be "beautiful" (since the gender of art is feminine or neutral in every language but our own) — "Virgin mother daughter of your son" — if we were to unthink everything, and I mean absolutely everything, on this blessed quotidian toilet. I think about a universal laxative. I think thoughts that go away. I think that I should hurry and liberate the "bathroom" from the stench of "creation." The secret — to remain in the form of the sunset — is to do it quickly, since, alas, I don't know, I believe it only takes a moment too long for that necessity to become a topsy-turvy pleasure and a final farewell, because it makes you feel like a mother. Malodorous creative-creature. You feel art, in that sense, which urges, which takes form — constipation or diarrhea — which ensures.

So, is the entire human universe a form of art? Not even in your dreams. The term "creation" is the privilege of the "artist," of the musician, poet, woman of ingenuity *&* finally: *maternity*.

For poor people it is only a...

The Homeric verses that so troubled Nietzsche:

> The gods gave humans pain so that the poets would have material to write about.

Hence, to the poet who is his own transition, to the sunset that I am, these verses smile while showing me: "maternity," "creativity," "certainty," a presumed-pensive stability that surrounds me, replete with absurd oddities, furious with liberation.

FRANCESCO SICILIANI AND "THE IDIOTS WITH FLASHES OF IMBECILITY"

The highly praised *"orchestral"* talents of my voice, by some music critics, would not pass a technical examination without a notion, even if approximative, of the *phonic instrumentation*, microphones and their resultant amplification, that I introduced to the theater in its greatest expression.

Microphones are in and of themselves musical instruments that we need to know how to play, especially when employing five or six of them at the same time.

Through such instruments (if they are connected to a mixer, with an equalizer, etc.) the voice can allow itself a musicality with truly unexpected aspects. The voice redresses, so to speak; it dresses itself to undress at its pleasure. It is capable of articulating the imperceptible, of performing harmony and modality and intervals just like an *"orchestra."* But, note, all this disrupts the "academic" technique of "projecting." For example, the technique of peremptory "portato" is prohibitive (it requires a release "without taking a breath" — to breathe is already to enunciate — if, indeed, you don't want to obtain a result of silly amplification, etc.). As a matter of fact, you need to take apart the "viva" voce as far as you can, but without forgetting about it. It is anything if not difficult, and it's no little thing if, in the end, you need to *not use* electronic equipment, but to *be it*: to be microphones, mixers, equalizers, dolby, *aphex*, *harmonizers*, etc.

That is what so many latecomer imitators, who unfortunately attempt to follow in my footsteps, fail to understand to their certain ruin in the summer squares.

Therefore, it is not enough: I *enunciate myself — I am the discourse* — even if I enunciate in a small room, with these instruments, meant for two people to listen, or no one at all. It is an entirely different universe that I like to claim kinship with, the Greeks and their rudimentary microphones. But with the pliers of the premise.

How can a theater critic fail to notice the carelessness, the mediocrity, the technical and mental flaws in the vulgar and obsessive reproduction of certain actors, whom it is not enough to limit oneself to detest, but is, rather, an aesthetic duty to confront and destroy?

Many years ago now ('77 — Rome — Teatro Quirino — *Richard III*), I had the honor to receive a visit in my dressing room from Maestro Francesco Siciliani who, being an enthusiast of the actor's *musicality*, invited me to discuss some *musical* projects with him.

I regret sacrificing in these pages my encounter with the maestro, which was so decisive for my research.

Siciliani proposed two opportunities, both of them, he noted, were "operatic." Two "dramatic poems" to stage *comme il faut*: *Manfred*, 5 acts by Lord Byron and a score by Schumann; & Ibsen's *Peer Gynt* along with a relevant score by Grieg.

The maestro entrusted me — carte blanche — with the adaptation, direction, sets, costumes, and the role of the protagonist in both cases. Production: Santa Cecilia. Performances at Rome's Teatro dell'Opera.

"Thank you from the bottom of my heart, Maestro, but I'm confused. Give me a night to think on it."

The next day, the final meeting. I explained that with *Othello* having already been launched for the same season, I would need him to allow me to stage only one of the two extraordinary pieces he had proposed, and this the following May. Intending to adapt & retranslate the texts, I chose the Byron-Schumann.

"But that's impossible, I beg you: unfortunately, the *Gynt* is already planned for the next Massenzio summer festival. I can't postpone it. Well, I guess that means we'll do a great *Manfred*" (which it was) "and we'll figure something out for the *Gynt*. Recommend an actor for me. Help me out…"

"There's…, Maestro!" I said, dissembling and rushing out the door.

Now, the greatest connoisseur of music and voice, religiously fasting from our home-grown "prose," failed to recognize the bad joke I made in my rash recommendation, and he gave the role to a certain tone-deaf actor, so that ill-fated *Gynt* was a complete failure.

I possess a recording that Piero Bellugi — the conductor of both *Manfred* and *Gynt* — made and that he sent me from Reggio Emilia, disoriented-amused, and documenting the inconceivable flop.

For the "*Manfred* project," I proposed a "new" formula to Siciliani, undoubtedly original: to realize that "privilege of damnation" in the *form of a concert*, by taking on the soloist playing all the "roles" as if they were evoked by the self-sorcerer, accentuating in this way the "heroism" of the author in a pathetic-parody, and by limiting the play to less than an hour, by introducing — for the first time *expressive* — *phonic instrumentation* in concert to accommodate Schumann's splendid music (subtracted from the servility of "the scenes") to take up the entire time of the performance (70 minutes total), by playing an (either/or not) harmonic fusion of the orchestra and of the words spoken by the soloist-author.

Sustained by an observant interlude of contoured and scattered light, a production such as this one would have constituted a performance solely on the rapport between Byron and Schumann, undisturbed by costumes, *décor*, wardrobe, hell fires, and idiotic furnishings. An extremely elegant sorcery.

This "formula" was more than an "inspired finding." If anything, it was the end of directorial findings that afflict the music at the opera.

Maestro Siciliani was a genius for having listened to me.

The experiment deserved an unprecedented triumph in this "genre" so degenerated, at the "opening," during the run, at the Scala, where we dared, amidst the strikes that were taking place among the chorus and orchestra, to make a live recording for Fonit Cetra, which is still available today, proving itself a miracle of the "market," even abroad.

In any case, the work elaborated in *Manfred* was the same as the procedure I used in *Othello*, which remained greatly admired and misunderstood, only because it was performed in a "prose" theater.

I've been in touch with the Enti Lirici on a daily basis ever since. My productions are presented, *naturaliter*, at the Scala, the San Carlo, the Comunale di Firenze, etc.

My much pursued and holy *indiscipline* (the surpassing of interdisciplinarity) is, for better or worse, fully repaid.

But let's return for a moment to that actor-"Gynt."

Siciliani, regardless of a "secret" pact that we made between us, had suggested the "key to the concert" to him so that at least the execution would be decent. Here is how everything that worked well in *Manfred* fell apart in that unfortunate performance (at Massenzio), which was managed by a vain and irresponsible parvenu.

Here is the ill-fated "prose," disassociated from Grieg's splendid music — both in and off the staff — here is how the notes debased themselves in dull movie music. The entrances-exits on stage plowing through the orchestra.

Here is Maestro Siciliani turning red with indignation at such ruin. And me, clearly joking this time: "How did it go, Maestro?"

"Let's just not talk about it, for the love of God, for the love of country... and the women, the women... those women... a mangy kennel. And that soloist... A donkey amidst the music! Enough! I want to do it again with you at the Scala..."

"So, we'll do it" (and, in fact, we would do it). "... Unfortunately, not this year; but I believe in *Gynt*. We'll do it again, the two of us."

And then there was Maestro Arrigo, the artistic director of Palermo's opera house: "*Gynt* with you, Carmelo, there's no question, but the fates recently castigated us with that off-key actor, a disaster. Like you, I want to redo it and do it right. But, you understand that *Peer Gynt* isn't *La Bohème*. It isn't possible to run it in two consecutive seasons. It'll have to wait."

But I just wanted to go away. I go away every time I breathe on stage. "And I don't go, and I don't stay."

I want to see even death bloom. I detest the cowardice of parroting. The subterfuge of identifying. I detest the "monstrosity of memory," and "Kean's amnesias." I abhor the flatulent and hackneyed theater that the subscribed critics like so well, enough to outlast them.

OPHELIA

Ophelia (we'll call the college girl who introduced herself to me thus) turns the lock two or three times on a traveling wardrobe-chest through which she entered and, circumspect, trembling, unfolds a sheet of paper and reads-looks at herself in the mirror.

Lili, for whom it was all a tempest of flashes, an empty stage being her little room — in greater and greater solitudes, she saw herself in the pages of Will(iam)'s universe... Ophelia reads and reads, disassociated from the maiden written there. Rummaging through the chests in the forbidden attic, she chose at random certain dead pages, for the love of habit, enchanted assiduousness, clumsily looking for her prince charming Hamlet. Lili is not a shameless person: certain quirks related to her age, this blossoming into a woman every second, the control of her own adolescent, or not, body that spent a lot of time, oh yes, before the mirror. Yes, but after having turned the key at least three times in the keyhole of the attic-amnesia of the Hamlet-little room, an unfortunate rosy girl like nearly all the others...

Ophelia rummages around in the heart of her beloved (O happiness!) through her own mirrored intimacy. O young woman reading, O the anxiety of lace & of lacework falling on the deaf floor of unreciprocated love!...

And her *saying*, that half-hearted saying, that failure to hazard kisses that she only gives herself in the page-mirror that apprises her of her body, of her face, of her eyes and *not of the other* — those Other's eyes are beautiful — yes, her *saying* cruelly disassociates itself from her gestures, which grow gradually more inattentive as she becomes more and more obstinate: and a comma is a misplaced hair, surprised nipples, those two dots, and her mouth that *says* is soon spoken by that little bit of lipstick that does not un-say.

O reading! O make-up!

Poor Ophelia! Poor Lili! So absorbed in your distraction. O mirrorings! You destroy yourself in the mirror, Lili; and those sleeping pages fall from between your hands (O your hands! O caresses!) Ah! The mirror confuses you, down there, on the deaf floor's ice of unreciprocated love…

> Oh, she's down there,
> as dark as the night is black!
> Alas, that life is a stupefying fair!

Ah! Lili, "so thin and so heroic!" A creature poorly mirrored and then never mirrored again! Stop crying those tears of yours! Leave your long hair alone! Don't disfigure yourself again! You see, the death preceptor entered your little room *&* now places you, drowned by a current cheap citation, on the blankets of water of a made-up bed, painted by Millais.

INCOMPREHENSION (TO LYDIA)

During my 12-year-old (boy-girl) childhood when it snowed and there was mulled wine, what a vacation-prize I received. I was transferred from the "fields" of Campi Salentina to Lecce — since on Sundays, people celebrated with the red at the Jesuits' Collegio Argento.

Oh, my Aunt Raffaella's large, beautiful, and neglected house, with its diverse garden full of gigantic figs and pomegranates, and peaches on the front balcony; round peaches that weighed as much as billiard balls, blood red both inside and out. Then there was the perfume of the climbing jasmine, which was so intense that all of us kids — my sister and three of our little cousins — slept with the window shut tight.

My aunt, who was an elementary school teacher in Maglie, was regret embodied, dressed in sheer, flowered nightgowns, persuaded as she was to have relinquished her quasi-artistic "sensibility" for the sake of the family. Some witnesses to her continual and rather nervous complaining: a black grand piano, utterly out of tune, in the empty living room that was replicated by an antique empire mirror; and, in the dining room, a dusty display cabinet with parsimonious shelves, empty burial recesses of never-interred volumes, or that were perhaps even lost gradually. A strange presence in this Alexandrian miniature of saintly ignorance that came close to desecrating the universe of the absent doctrine — a truly strange presence indeed — was the near entirety of the complete works, uneven & pitted little volumes of "Bibi" Shakespeare from the first edition by Rusconi, dozing in the autumn of their life.

Likewise, the music scores for voice and piano by Tosti, Toselli, and a bunch by Verdi, were all piled up in a heap at the base of the floor-length mirror and were sleeping in the music room. It's true that there are certain sunsets that will never return, because as soon as the disillusionment of adolescence raises its bewildered head from the floor of childhood, the last sunset is already in sight.

"You're off-key," my aunt of a ghost said, growing angry, who absolutely had to accompany me on the piano.

"I don't know what to tell you."

So, she would start to sing softly. We had not been graced with the gift of harmony: the two of us and all the yellow and black keys, without exception.

I would keep my mouth shut while she despaired over her "Caro Ideale" who never returns, and sneak off to the Stratford-room, where, like a troglodyte, I read in indisputable incomprehension the verses of Apemantus in *Timon of Athens*, my first love in poetry-theater.

I said "incomprehension," and life has only now taught me that there is nothing else that pacifies us

INCOMPREHENSION (TO LYDIA)

in our adult anguishes, be they artistic or not, be they "pensive" or not — not love accords, not rare attempts at friendship, not the attentions that we duly mistreat; not the approval and caring of the "reciprocal," the eternally disillusioned "agreements" — nothing in this world is as comforting to us as incomprehension, pathetic, a bit awkward, for those who surround us. Assiduous.

How else could we survive several lustra of "devoted" love, the alternating seasons of shimmering moods in the decades of a single day, the disputes, the truces, the neurotic *maquillage*, the coming and going in the room where time is slow and brief despite the moderate, intolerable tolerance; if she, lady incomprehension, never invoked, were not watching with us and over us.

What would our plans be, if, immediately "understood" by those around us, they were to result in satisfaction, if achieved before having been undertaken? What would our life be, if already lived.

So, that amazed way of mine to read Shakespeare between the lines, beyond the literal sense, applauded, unconscious, my child's mind which by that text was thought out syllable by syllable, one word after another, then two and three together, devoid of purpose, sovereign in and of themselves, fatuous vertical small fires, powerless to arrange themselves in sequence-ranks in the sentence. In my then ignorance, it wasn't that I would be enticed by some candid oratorical vein of hyperbole and the inevitable seriousness in infantile nonsense. I was reciting without the vessel of a concept. The luminescent, white flowers of the climbing jasmine would open up in the evening, the green of the hedges fading to black, and the walls of the house vanishing, if seen from the vegetable garden, as soon as the lights were turned on inside.

I would read aloud softly, in no way embarrassed by my inability to understand anything at all; words, sounds, wanderers by nature, like the stars above, arranged here and there in the sky, spelled out in clumps, but rare in the face of myriad other scattered teardrops.

"The signified is a rock in the mouth of the signifier." Do such precocious childhoods exist? If so, then there's no need to grow up, my sweet companion (in) comprehension. So much so that old Werther, who commits suicide in order to avoid regressing, old Werther's young labor pains started when he had not yet even met his Lotte. We grow up. At school, *&* precisely in the hour devoted to "poetry," they teach you to turn the puerile delirium of a line of verse into antiquated prose. They ask you for a mundane phrasal "precision," with the excuse that it is to ascertain if you "understand" what you are reading; it is, in reality, the liberty of the verse that they mean to reduce to squalid commentary. The "what it means" usurps the sovereignty of the "how it is said." From this point, the "story" of poetry supplants the "toilsome" verses without story. As it is, the "tradition" is always understood as not what it was when it was alive, but how it presents itself now that it is dead. And this *it never was* — if it truly was alive — is taken as a certainty. We exorcise the past by defrauding it from the *present* that was.

Just like the sanctimonious cemetery that is reserved for the "classics," even in theater. Whoever the lunatic is that assures their revival and restores them intact to today's readers is a distinguished intellect, seemingly a guarantor of philological reverence and devotion, that imbecile! And whoever, on the contrary, is a wanderer in love with everything that it is (and this is impossible), everything that it *was*, infuses life into it, forestalling its comforting mortality, and revives and rewrites those dead gestures and sounds regardless of the dust, and in the *rewriting* exhibits the entirety of his very own *discomfort of being there*; yes, this person is considered a brigand, a profaner of the universal patrimonial cemetery; a thief.

Whoever museumifies the present with piles of bones from times past is "trustworthy," "serious." The lack of discipline, however, in he who, oblivious to the centuries, lives in the present — that which the *present* was — is a "disease-spreader" or a *Scapigliato bricoleur*, to put it in the kindest possible terms.

Never mind what happens then to *he who does not know who he is* and nevertheless grapples with *that which no one knows what had been*. This is "my case." The scene of absence, which does not mean not being there, but rather its breathlessness and disenchantment, in the act of denouncing myself outside of every "role." Everything else that surrounds me is shameless, recidivist absconding, a chewer of corpses, rhetorical, oratorical — the little cadaver's foul breath, indeed — ostentatious *&* unwieldly vitality. Rounded exuberance of the collective com-pass of the masses.

I am certain of this: when, a few centuries from now (I'll not be suffering from any Mayakovskian victim complexes), the living will read these notes of mine, they will feel my presence among them (above all, those who are absent). You, however, who are alive by chance, who spit on the life that *was*; you arrogant interpreters (not only of the putrefied past, but also of the (no longer) codified present), you will never be. Only who is *missing* is and, therefore, returns.

But let's return to my boy-girl childhood self's Will, while my aunt, inspired, yearned for her "Caro Ideale" who never returned to her, croaking and playing on the black and yellow keys, with the scent of flowers in the air. That carefree mental quiet of the sounds; that innocent ignorance of the "plot," which aroused no curiosity; that avoidance of staccato tones, regard-

INCOMPREHENSION (TO LYDIA)

less of whoever may be speaking in the scene. It all resembled Verdi's music — all country, family in the libretti — but more beautiful, less beautiful, incomprehensive of the "plots," notwithstanding the "good guys" and the "bad guys."

"O terra addio!" Aunt Raffaella-Aida was exaggerating in her room, while I eulogized Timon's death in mine. We were in harmony; it was excessive, inconclusive. Yes indeed, you need a structure, a rigor, that's right, but by no means oblivious of our incoherent little concert taking place in two separate rooms of our minds and of our senses dazed from the jasmine. There was a — "textual" — misunderstanding, more profound *&* happy than every "know-it-all" to come. Who cares about Verdi, Tosti, Shakespeare. Not even they were themselves. What was missing was there in that sunset.

What matters for me as an actor on stage today is that the "pre-established" end remembers to be so only in that principle. And then it forgets.
 There, we perform on ourselves the Will that is within us. It is up to him to make do with the nonsense that names us. It is in this way that we shake his Will that he *was*. Adapting ourselves to who he was, by parroting his verses, in the "modernization" of the "conflicts," is to deny him the present-day stage and ourselves the life of his past.

A PROSE STAGE (GIUSEPPE DI STEFANO)

One afternoon — I was 15 years old — a family friend escorted me along the little streets of tuff from the baroque period around Lecce, to the little temple where Maestro Barbara lived. He was a refined connoisseur of voice and had accompanied Tito Schipa in concert.

Gifted with a great voice but an indulgent throat, had I been a tenor, I would have sounded like certain unpleasant voices without a "center," that, unbearable in the "phrasing," allow you to win over the unrefined audience with "alarms!"

My chaperon had waited, prudently, in the hall. The audition-performance began. Music? No sir, I didn't know squat about reading music.

"It doesn't matter, perhaps it's even better. You can do it," & he lightly touched the finely tuned keys, inviting:

Rispetta almen le ceneri
Di chi moria per te.

Donizetti was dead, and that crime could have been carried out to the bitter end. Even though I lived in "Campi Salentini," a place that remains disconnected from the rest of the world still today, ever since I can remember, melodrama was master of our household, either on the radio — not the horrible audio on television sets, which were unthinkable at the time, thank heavens — or sometimes, at the theater: the Politeama in Lecce, the Petruzzelli in Bari, Rome, Verona and other tourist destinations: these were precious occasions to listen to voices that we don't hear anymore. Di Stefano, Pertile, Neri, Simionato, Taddei and so on in silence. In other words, for me theater was "opera": sounds, lights, splendor, extravagant waste, a performance where, first and foremost, people didn't talk like they did in real life. Two or three times, I attended performances with "prose" actors. To my young ear, these people seemed to grumble among themselves, so great was their "unaffectedness," they arranged, so to speak, to come to an agreement on who would have to "start" the song that wasn't coming. I was surprised that the audience applauded actors who hadn't even attempted to perform a "recitative."

"When will they sing?" I asked my grandmother, pestering her.

"Ignoramus. These ones don't sing, they talk."

"They're paid for talking?"

"Why wouldn't they be? Do you want them to talk for free?"

"But this is the same theater where we come to hear music and singers."

"That's enough! These ones don't have anything to do with music. They can't sing."

A PROSE STAGE (GIUSEPPE DI STEFANO)

"So, why on earth did we come here?" I couldn't wrap my head around it. It still seemed to me like the people on stage were coming to an agreement between themselves. "But if they're talking about their own business, why don't they speak more quietly? We can hear everything they're saying!"

"Ignoramus! Ignoramus! I wonder what will become of you when you're a man. And thanks to you I can't understand what's going on."

"But why do you care, if it's their business?"

"What do you mean 'their business'?" And then my grandmother expressed her irritation in Leccese dialect. "Let's go!" she said and rose from her seat. "Saturday night there's Aureliano Pertile. Let's go now, I said. You can't understand these things."

Indeed, I didn't understand them, & more than 30 years have passed, and I still don't understand "those things."

Then there was the nausea of the shaky-vibrato-bombastic "bel canto"; the dominion of the polyphonic *lied*, which we found mortifying (a closed voice as base requirement), would not have hindered me from appreciating the "centrality" of Domingo, the "supremacy" of Callas, the "velvet smoothness" of Ettore Bastianini, certain things by Carreras who, in his "colors," evokes the only melodramatic love of my life: the unparalleled voice of Giuseppe Di Stefano.

And, 30 years after "those things," in Milan, it is Di Stefano who is naturally "Pippo" because he is naturally "musical."

"I am the Carmelo Bene of opera." Pippo amused himself by keeping "music" at a distance. "I don't know what to do with music. The staff is stuff for tenors."

So, he would be appropriately yearning, while his 24-year-old voice was seducing me in *Lucia* on the gramophone. It is Di Stefano's colors, his phrasing, that make him a musical, winged "breath"; truly, the music is not enough to contain it. His Sicilian cart drivers' dirges are so much more brilliant than opera (without quotation marks) could express. Divine grace. What did I have in "common" with De Stefano? Here we go: the innate musicality, the "centrality," the "colors," the first-rate "intention," the 120 Gitanes daily, the sense of the empty orchestra pit — and that of life as a waste.

"One tenor less, thank God!" An expert, Maestro Barbara's comment was ruthless in response to Donizetti's massacre. I knew it from the start. But what should I do then? I would need to leave the "Campi Salentini" right there where they were. But what should I do?

"Why don't you become an actor!" That's my bizarre cousin for you.

"An actor? Do you mean like those people who stand on stage for two hours in front of an audience trying to come to some agreement, and who never sing?..."

"Yeah, like that. What's wrong with that?"

SALVADOR DALÌ

*We're tired
of this feeling of guilt...*

Who are we? Those three or four people who don't belong in this world. Oh wretchedness! Where are you Saint Genet? Where are you, transgressor of transgression? You knew how to adore a policeman and not give a damn about the antimony from your country's *comédie*. A thief and squanderer of liberty.

I like to imagine our life in the role of that character in uniform, who in your "screens" dies, struck by an enemy bullet at the very moment he settles in to take a crap.

David Harali, the photographer-sorcerer of comatose war victims, really missed an opportunity there. What an invented reality *this* life is!

How grotesque the elegance of the exquisite archer in the act of releasing his arrow seems in relation to he who is struck by that very same arrow.

It's simple: you need only grip the bow the wrong way around, pull it toward your chest *&* not take aim. Then the arrow pierces you, without further ado, there where the arrogance of common sense doesn't expect it.

It's a purposeful way of making-unmaking, invoking the obscene. A way of closing our mouths in order to scream.

Then we reopen our wide-open lips anew after a forced yawn had contorted them into a spasm, and we remain like that, without emitting a sound, until we become our very own constant grimace.

Eroticism is worthless, prenatal language. To go beyond it is to venture into the stillness that resembles that other kind of rest, the stillness of the dead.

However, it is not enough to simply step off the path. We are not satisfied with planting the plan's seed. Straying from the path to find shelter in the desert, far from desires and urges, gone with the wind at first and then without wind, the chest's sails deflated, arms lifeless-shrouds, truncated by the damage of being carefree. In a state of agitation, the *obscene* smiles on us; it does not smile at us, to avoid an unpleasant loss of teeth falling on the floor due to pyorrhea, to not move the suspension of the journey.

The time for racking our brains is past, whether it was men who invented the "rules of courtship" for the French ladies from Provence, or if it was precisely the ladies themselves who contrived those necessities.

Ah! Don Jose, ah(y) Gasset, ah Ortega!

It is no longer a question of women and men. In the end, it is *pornography*. Yes, the very same pornography as in Franz Kafka's trials; that fear of the law thus dispossessed from consciousness in stupor (not eroticism as Bataille intended it: the supreme component of the game that was Franz Kappa's nothingness).

That way of wasting our life, our day in the sun, by standing in an open doorway and posing questions that have already been answered, to the irony of (simulated) desire, to make a big spectacle at the hour (and the hour is always) of closing time.

O impeded questions, unspeakable truth.

"... I was covered in spit. It could have been roses. It wouldn't cost any more if it were happiness..."

A scene that *suspends* the nauseating quarrel of the *"tragic"* is above all *absurd*, an unthinking oblivion of Eros. It is *obscene* in its exceeded Eros. It is obscene in its *pornography*: "Look, my dear Carmelo" (Dalì, who was pointing his finger at the figure of a lively orgy at our feet), "our indifference in watching is divine. When it comes to producing it for ourselves, we only need to cast a few humans."

I was staring at that scene of nothingness with love and heard the painter, Salvador's *aceitunada voz*.

Salvador who read to me — improvised the affront of a thought: "Lorca... No! *Il voulait seulement m'inculer!...*"

Then what can be staged? Well this morbid curiosity, if you want, if you can, about things that we know. This pathetic, uninspired, consideration. This making of discourse without reply. ("Even laughter wants to be heroic"). This oblivious moving away amplified in the saying. Deafening and dispassionate, like the poor wildflowers of drowned Ophelia depicted floating on the water's surface. Awash with madness if, indeed, "Pray you, love, remember."

Indeed, let's drown her once and for all, this painted Ophelia, on stage, one image too many, from the moment that my vocation is and always will be to *unstage the play*.

I don't know how to "stage a play." Someone asks the "property master," usually from the dressing room: "Did you "set the stage?" That's what it is, a job truly meant for a property master and today assigned to people with talented hair, like Strehler, Squarzina, etc., in other words, to the director. Perhaps they do it in the Stabili theaters to save on the cost of hiring a "property master," a profession which is becoming more & more rare, as opposed to the plethora of directors.

Let's return to "unstaging the play." An "inspired idea"? I would say, rather, a "lost idea." Not to be confused with the "traviata," that fallen woman, because I was once a "traviata" in the wretchedness of my list.

"Il faut toujours avoir une seule idée, cher Carmelo," he felt compelled to say to me 10 years ago in another of our stupendous meeting-matches at the Hôtel Meurice in Paris. Dalì again, with whom, at the time, I was meant to collaborate on a *Don Quixote* with Eduardo that RAI then found — they said — "unpopular" (*sic*).

Dalì had just seen a private screening, dedicated to him, of *Our Lady of the Turks*, a 1968 film, or better yet, the "anti-1968 film" par excellence, misunderstood to the bitter end.

At the end of the screening, Dalì was enthusiastic: "*Fort bien, fort bien, c'est Dalinien!*"

Da-lì [from there] we went on to talk about genius and the artist. We started to argue endlessly. Between one knee-bending and another. Someone kept rapping on the door, enter Captain Moore, a former officer whom Dalì had taken out of retirement and engaged as his servant-secretary, with the understanding that he retain his Irish uniform. In fact, he served him in his old captain's uniform, without his stripes, which he could no longer display.

Between raps on the door, Dalì was waiting for who knows which of his mistresses, perhaps the "lost one." First, he got down on his knees: "*Excuse-moi*, Carmelo"; they were still rapping on the door: "*Entrez*," and Captain Moore appeared in the doorway; he was holding a large bouquet of red roses that the *concierge* must have just delivered, who knows who they were from.

So, between a bunch of red roses and a "lost" love, Dalì left me with this bit of wisdom, "No, you cannot be a genius yet, I understood that from your film... There is still too much suffering... You're still an artist, but I'm a genius."

Today, I understand how right Dalì was to predict and to teach me, at the height of the 70's, how "genius" goes beyond "suffering." Here, we return to the concept of "hero," but even greater in his *loss*, because "abandoned," because more crippled and weaker.

I APPEARED TO THE MADONNA

DANTE IN BOLOGNA 7-31-81

Never, in my previous lives had I been permitted to perform-disappear, perched like a bursting flower on high, facing furnace blasts from the auxiliary lights in that sweltering heat (at Asinelli, the tower), facelessly orating to the mania of more than 100,000 people, down there, at my feet, a densely packed crowd in adoration. The night in the skies had already clothed itself with the insufferable summer night's streaks of dull gray and black.

Zangheri, the erudite city's first citizen Renato, had long since condemned me to sing Allegheri's work on that date (the anniversary of the tragic massacre) in the presence of the people who would have had to think back on that terrible event, as is fitting to secular remembering, better than in a rather distracted remembrance in San Petronio — a poetic occasion to facilitate a thoughtful memory — before the parody of the present were to supplant the last tragedy.

Now, it so happened that more than a month before the soon to be historic, planned Dantean celebration, the indiscreet *Resto del Carlino*, tempted and bilked from many sides, was waving around from the tops of its columns ominous headlines to their readers, relating the political *&* catholic-secular discontent of the council in charge of proper civic duties.

In short, the experience of the reddest socialist carnations was in tune with the sacristy's Catholic chrysanthemums in condemning the psalms from "comedy," too many merrymakers, in their opinion, and therefore incapable of paying homage mournfully — it was befitted as it was befitting — to that sorrowful event, to be consumed, if anything, in holy felicity and solitude, with each person contemplating it while sitting around a table. To hell with the public square!

Unfortunately, in the heart of the city council's crusades, the motive was elsewhere.

Bologna's *Il Resto del Carlino* — lacking in scholarly obligations and always on vacation — had revealed to the God-fearing people, who for years had resided in the Palazzo D'Accursio, besieged, God only knows by what, that even though the poet in question was the greatest craftsman of our Italian idiom, he had been in his lifetime an ill-tempered man. He deemed no one in Bologna worthy of paradise and had condemned to hell those "Knights of Our Lady," calling them ruffians and guarantors, who were particularly adept at running public affairs. Still, it wasn't enough, because there's inferno and then there's inferno, just like there's decorum and decorum. In fact, that odious Tuscan's slanderous quill damned those spirits to hell in a rather unpleasant bolgia once *&* for all. He had nailed them down in the miry depths and sprayed them with huge, unequivocal, as well as everlasting, quantities of shit.

What if during that very same festive mourning, rather than thinking about the previous year's massacre, a spritely cricket were to insinuate in no matter which one of the cracks in the speaker's skull, to shout at the violent winds a few verses extorted from that unedifying bolgia in which we find the aforementioned atrocity, denouncing to the entire city even this other, extraneous, 7th-centenary recurring event?

Here we have in a nutshell the reason for the cautiousness that incited the Knights Templar to raise their shields, opposing in open sally Don Renato's "disregard," who in exposing them, these successors of the "Knights of Our Lady," to public ridicule was putting at risk both the reputation of their holy order & his own title of "Don."

I found myself the innocent victim of their private squabbles. A certain Bendinelli — who, among other things, was, in that period, meant to be joined in holy, but contested, matrimony to a liberal woman, a lineage contentious for those white-flowered crusaders, which also stank of heresy: it was an exhausting delay judging by the betrothed's age — his zeal disproportionate to what the circumstances warranted, was disrupting their consensus, threatening to remove them from their seats and to throw the red Socialist carnations out. In reality, the Socialists were not at all afraid, but rather determined to proceed with a blind war against the most vermillion Don Renato.

Reckless as they were, they joined with the sacristy's Catholics to prevent me from vociferating the offensive poetry that, from what people were saying, was preparing to be even more iniquitous, seeing as how my voice would resonate in not just one location, but rather throughout the whole of Bologna, thanks to a complicit device that had been fabricated to magnify the sound.

Additionally, much to their dismay, they had learned from their trusted spies that a wagonful of other such devices was making its way from RAI's Roman fortress. Undoubtedly the work of the devil, if these devices were even capable of broadcasting all across Italy that heretical & perverse attack that was being prepared in the city.

They considered it, therefore, appropriate and necessary to entreat the governor of that fortress to spare the people of Bologna such a far-reaching echo of their "past" infamies and, in all contempt, that might possibly be reenacted by means of that scoundrel of a worthless poet. So, they were asking if it might be possible to avoid informing the entire world about that which threatened to make a twofold Simonist anniversary come true.

In this way, even in Rome, there was turmoil.

The interim governor holding the office for the summer summoned the most heroic of his surviving sergeants, mercenaries under the command of various divisions to decide the fate of the Emilian city on that occasion. Here crosses and carnations arrived at a rather strange understanding: yes, the fatal device would have broadcasted on a gigantic scale — both audio and video — that *Lectura Dantis* from the tower, not only in the Italian regions, but also in "neurovision"; however, this operation would have taken place the day following that event in Bologna, that is to say, in a "deferred" time. In other words, the curious angst, estranged and uncultivated, would have been satisfied a day later.

I wasn't present at that meeting, but I was aware that the various obstinate parties came with daggers drawn in my defense and in defense of Don Renato, opposing the truly strange idea of "deferring" that tale, which was undoubtedly a herald of the civic *&* municipal good sense of those plebs.

The heat raged on. I was laying down like someone about to pass away in a rather expensive cell of a Bolognese hospice, known as Crest, outside the city. To mitigate the nuisance of passing away, I had soaked the rugs with cold water, and was tiredly holding two bewitched contraptions, overused to communicate from afar, to my ears. In truth, they constituted a rather complex communication bridge that made it possible to listen and to communicate with the studio located on a street nearby, Via delle Calzolerie, and from there with the stands at the Torre Asinelli, which had been fermented by the sound sappers who toiled in the sun — as if by magic, in the space of a single morning, a special crew with the assistance of the local firemen had erected more than one ferrous-wood tower with specific battering rams, to fortify our voice — who tested the sounds of thunder, the tones, and the perception and intensity for the occasion, since the sun was setting and it was necessary to conquer the enemy factions, &, on the other hand, to elicit a great torment in the hearts of the people listening.

In the afternoon, those specialized sappers were atop the scorching stands, not at all fazed by the uproar coming from the crowds below, and using the devices to follow the recommendations of the expert positioned in the aforementioned studio. The expert was called Salvatore Maenza. He was blind in both eyes, and therefore an adept master of music, not to mention the inventor of tried and true, effective loudspeakers capable of diffusing any sort of hostile dialectic resistance with ear-splitting noise if necessary. First, I chose this creator and, then, Don Renato charged him with assisting me in taking the city from within; both Piazza Maggiore and Santo Stefano were prepared to receive Allegheri's cantos, as long as he stayed in constant contact with me, always swearing passionately.

As soon as it started getting dark, I caught up with those valiant sappers of mine at the top of the stands; the sawbones supported and comforted me. My gaze fell between the tower's merlons, and it offered me a sight I had never seen before, an ocean of polychromatic people.

I asked one of the cops on duty how much time was left before my part was to begin, and he told me an hour, or a little less.

A southerly wind kicked up, and it was beating the hell out of the megaphones that had been raised on pikes. I forced myself to keep the spirits at bay and to calm myself down, like boxers do before a fight.

It was time. I clambered up the ladder's rickety rungs and finally showed myself to the crowd, which was perhaps more amazed at its own immensity than it was at my mirage, and which welcomed the end of the wait through my appearance. An indescribable roar of applause resounded from far off public squares and in all the surrounding streets.

I appeared. With my eyes closed in front of the luminescent music stand, I began to sing Allegheri's verses. But from elsewhere, in the time of snow and mulled wine from my childhood. Then I faded away, & the canto followed as if proffered by ser Boccaccio in that very same place 700 years earlier.

The sounds chased after one another above the rooftops, and the people's devout silence created an enchantment that made my fading away even more sweet.

A new blossoming of the mind, a Marian devotion, at the feet of my favorite silvery Madonna clothed in amnesiac blue and pink.

Now, I say myself, while I had been said, a chance to hear as I had never been afforded at any other time in my life, while that prayer of mine was slowly losing itself, and while my saying's silence gradually forgot its sense, Our Lady, retreating, was vanishing from my enamored gaze. Since my child-like thinking could not persuade itself that he, himself, was the Madonna who had been invoked. Because the Madonna seemed blessed to me, as I addressed her and was saying piously. I was *speaking to her*, but *I wasn't that saying. I saw her.* Evoked, the mirage persisted, until newly *oblivious, I continued to say my own discourse*, and the vision disappeared into the discourse, from which my prayer — I understand now — had expelled her.

There was (there is), therefore, *an appearance of the voice* that always verifies itself if you confer w i t h, if you speak *to*.

> When I began to make hearing
> useless...

the voice was saying to me, my internal singing the listening, and, ventilated by a migraine's wing, my mind sank into the south of the South of the saints from elsewhere; but unthought, like a delicate hot-air balloon at the mercy of the heavens on the boundlessness of the tired sea:

"There are idiots who have seen the Madonna, and there are idiots who have not seen the Madonna... Seeing or not seeing the Madonna; that's the theme..."

"Saint Giuseppe da Copertino, a swine herder, gave himself wings by frequenting his own ineptitude, and at night, while praying, he reached the altars of the Virgin, flying with his mouth hanging open."

"The idiots who see the Madonna have unexpected wings..."

"The idiots who don't see the Madonna don't have wings. They can't fly at all, and yet they fly anyway, &, instead of landing, they fall down again, like some guy with blocks tied around his feet, who wants to untie them, but instead he decides to cut off his feet."

"But those who see don't see what they see; those who fly are themselves the flight. He who flies is unaware of it. Such a miracle annihilates them: more than seeing the Madonna, they are the Madonna they see... If you want to embrace someone, you are the intercourse; when you kiss, you are the mouth..."

"But the idiots who see the Madonna don't really see her, like two eyes staring at two eyes through a wall: transparency is the miracle. Madness is the sacrament, because blind faith closed these eyes; it transformed the strata — the strata were made of rock — it transformed them into veils. And the eyes saw sight. Either man is blind in this way, or God is objective…"

Giuseppe Desa, the saint, was extremely fond of a particular painting of the Virgin in the Grottella Monastery. She was so dear to him that one day he disowned his own mother — that poor, foolish woman who was even more illiterate than her son — "You're not my mother. You're not my mother!" Then he pointed to the image, "She's my mother!"

He had been seen levitating on numerous occasions while on his knees in front of that image. Troglodyte, he would utter a blessed nothing. So, an animalistic howl and flight. Who knows where he landed: on the cornice of the town church, or on the branch of an olive tree. Asleep.

No one in this world had the ability to wake him, with the exception of his superior, who, being a Franciscan, instructed him of the rule: "Obedience, eh?" (What a careless prior he was to clumsily put Giuseppe's life in jeopardy, given that he was aware of the precariousness of his enraptured state.)

"I'm sleepin', I'm sleepin', what d'ya want from me!" Giuseppe, unfortunate and obedient, woke up and, having realized the unsteady state of his body, suffering from vertigo, prayed for a ladder while crying.

From flight to flight, he was transferred (on foot, which was the Holy See's punishment-penance), after a brief sojourn in Naples, during which the bored court distracted itself with one of his concocted "evolutions," when in Osimo, he obstinately implored the Vatican that he might be granted the opportunity to see his beautiful Madonna again, the one he had abandoned in the monastery in Copertino. A grace that was long denied and then, suddenly, who knows why, granted.

Well, when the longed-for celestial image was delivered to him, "I don't want it anymore," he said.

A caprice? Quite the contrary. The fact was that Giuseppe Desa "Openmouthed" had little by little unmasked the painter of that Madonna of his: Malatasca (in this way he named the devil).

So, the Devil and the image. *A sin of worship*.

Sight is prayer's hell. *Sight* is a *deficiency* of *saying*.

Speaking (to) the Madonna. This parenthesis is the abyss. How sorry should we feel for an actor — the most talented deliriously de-generate — when recalling the dubious nature of addressing the saying *to*, if love's banquet is love of saying, if conversing is only the listening of he who names.

How loathsome (the alternative to "laic" in Tommaseo's dictionary) is the theater of repeat performances.

It is madness to try to entertain the Madonna. She is that nothingness of which we are made. And if the voice expropriates her, makes *her appear*, it is because we pray *devoutly*.

Devotion is that miserable torment from which our prayer gasps and dies, and, grieving — a melancholy consequence — the Madonna *appears to us*.

Mortified in rumors, our voice has its *visions*. It is these visions that the *musical saying* reconverts in the voice's dark implosion, such that we speak *the* Madonna. Our Lady of the blessed failures:

> From the sweet lyre crowning the lovely sapphire
> whose grace ensapphires the heaven's brightest
> sphere: I am angelic love encompassing…

As I was saying. I appeared. It is an indescribable — something entirely different from the reflective past — passive verb. I am said. I am, myself, that Lady.

> With this the circling melody was sealed,
> and all the other lights within that sphere
> sang out the Blessed Virgin Mary's name.

The end of the Lectura Dantis met with thunderous applause, (un)founded on enthusiasm. Without a doubt, *I had appeared to the Madonna*.

Alas, it is not enough to escape from the image; like that way Epictetus had of talking to himself in his ear "in the middle of the market," eternally-returning, since to disappear is nevertheless the only paradoxical formula of appearing to the ear of other people.

"The altars move toward them (the saints)," machinated by psychotic feeble-mindedness in the crowd. It's a miracle (all of them are miracles) *of the public square*.
We appear to *Madonna the public square*.

It is the crowd of the miraculously healed inasmuch as it is confronted with a listening that is not its own, without the remedy of the reply, excluded from the discourse and only *&* always, for that reason, *moved*.

It is thus that we appear to the Madonna. *Sub specie spectaculi*.

Saying the listening brought about a certain religious concentration, by means of exclusion, in the human sea, which, for this reason, was transformed into a crowd of worshippers. You are adored, in the fading listening, no longer in the haven of naming, drowned out by applause, the only delayed reply granted to the faithful, and shows them to you in the blessed vanity of "many thanks" and kisses.

We appear to the Madonna subjectified by the exultant crowd.

In this way, *The Madonna has her visions*. Mass hallucinations in which Our Lady, demoted to a mirage, encounters her fatal *prostitution*.

What other era, if not our own, so characteristic of "consumption," can promise perpetual miracles.

The senseless oversaturation of the image-making (television-cinema) market is, not by chance, a predictable impediment to the mirage.

For a miracle to occur, you need to disappear in the saying. While *the phoné's appearance* says its very own paradox, as a mass "elsewhere" of the discourse.

This Madonna that I am no longer is forced to the brothel of images in gratifying the crowds. She is condemned to be seen. She is applauded, demoted to the friendly "encore" of one night's paradise on earth.

Nothing remains, if *from nothing* we appear to the Madonna.

"THOSE WHO SEE, DON'T SEE WHAT THEY SEE…"

We have arrived at our "heroic," so-called cinematographic, parenthesis. A cycle of *dépense*. An enormous waste of energy in the adventure to venture making no fewer than five consecutive films: directed, produced, cinem-idiot-ographied, decorated, wardrobed, fitted, acted-directed five films "d'auteur," the author of his own unique undoing. People wanted to know how, in one lifetime, I successfully completed five films, which should have taken at least five lifetimes to make.

Cinema parenthesis and splendor of sublime acts of foolishness that were actually strewn in the land of the South: Lydia-Madonna, beset by the native people of Otranto's devotion. Lydia, made-up to look sacred, who devoured her sandwiches and chugged her beverages on the set, which was composed of only me — actor, author, set designer, wardrobe master, director, producer, and first, second, and third camera — and Mario Masini, from Siena, who was an extraordinary cameraman, assistant focus-puller, gaffer, and a whole team of best boys in one. Lights: 13 spots, along with a pre-war 7-kilowatt generator, which we used to inundate Otranto's church and its immense mosaic with light. That was at least for the first, risky cinematographic event.

Why cinema?

People have always clumsily misunderstood that I was beating an avant-gardist path of image against word, even before I filmed myself or I filmed the impossibility of filming anything other than the set, even at the beginning of my theatrical debuts.

I attempted to repudiate this through five films wherein *silence* reigns and *logos* is decidedly excluded.

Cinema: realm of images. I attempted to go beyond the image in order to dispel the misunderstanding surrounding my prior adventure in theater. Cinema: the subject's game that plays perversely with the image, as we do with the most trivial of toys. The camera lens played like a kaleidoscope for children who in their astonishment hear something entirely different, the musicality of the images, the optical effects of the *phoné*. Instead of the story, this *bricolage* of sounds and images is intended to be a citation of the story, this myriad of signs adrift of the sound wave that dictates the movement. Everything played in perfect a-synchronous, in the idiosyncrasy between "musicality" and "music," which are not always the same thing.

So, *Our Lady of the Turks*, if you like.

Dressed up as "cinéma-vérité," *Our Lady of the Turks* was not understood as a grandiose epic poem on the "south of the South of the saints," much less as cinematographic language.

In the same way as with the preceding novel of the same name, nothing was understood from such a grandiose parody of interior life.

I confronted a certain use of the image in cinema that I had previously rejected and that I found intolerable: a decadent, tributary cinema, a provincial literary cinema, where what matters is the believability of the plot, the articulation of the *logos*, etc., etc.

Our Lady of the Turks did not yet deserve the prodigious editing techniques later used in *Don Giovanni* (4000 frames) or in *Salome* (4500 frames in less than an hour of film). It also didn't deserve other, rather important things. We had measured out the film, because we were there on the pretext that we would be filming three short films. We shot the film in 16mm, which we miraculously enlarged to 35mm. We made due with scrapped film, and with the scraps we added images with no adornments, in the name of my now, classic method (?) that adds in order to subtract. We tended toward excess as we de-colored the image itself.

It was this unadorning the adorned that constituted my first film. But we are always on our first film. We are always on our first verse; we are always on our first line. We are always at "the first," as I like to remind myself.

The "exteriors" were filmed with olive and fig trees that we replanted in the bedroom of my Arab house that faced the Sticchi's kitsch Moorish villa.

Conversely, the "interiors," that is to say the moments of reflection, of solitude, the bedroom, the kitchen, all took place in the public square, in the Piazza di Santa Cesarea Terme, located precisely at the heart of the provincial road that went from Otranto — by way of Maglie — to Lecce.

It's easy to imagine the difficulties of filming with a camera that is always "zoomed in." We had only one Arriflex that was always hidden & camouflaged. The injections for protecting the liver were conducted in religious apprehension in the center of the public square, with the truly devout cops' complicity. They would block the traffic coming from both Otranto and from Maglie. In this way, chaotic traffic jams formed almost immediately, and the drivers were certainly not pleased to find themselves in Lourdes, but rather eager to get the hell out of there.

A few days before, the town's mayor had rightly reprimanded the infuriated plebs, who were informed that they would remain in the dark for at least the next two months because of a fireworks scene. And eternity is summer. The Christian Democrat mayor, an elementary school teacher, who was extremely understanding, tossed no less than 685 complaints in the trash, so they would not reach the police commissioner in Lecce, who had already been asked to "look the other way." The mayor, a very spirited man, showed the kids who was boss by walking all over them and reprimanding the unruliest ones with slaps in the face, all the while singing like a crazy person. He had dealt with the plebs who were without lights in the same heroic manner, when they were threatening to never vote for him again, and by way of example, he got down on his knees & said: "This is how we kneel before art!"

Meanwhile, the haloed Lydia-Madonna in the heavens was perpetually and precariously perched in a fig tree, surrounded by flowers of gold, azure, and red streamers, falling streamers, and was demanding to come down.

Disturbances occurred involving halted marching bands, saint's festivals stopped at midpoint, delayed and deviated buses due to the presence of a small table adorned with black and gold, like in a funeral mass. Then there was the ungodly bus driver who was chasing after me to kill me. If only he had known that I was thinking about the Puccinian intermezzo from *Manon* while I was running, he would most certainly have caught up with me.

Like a benedictory muezzin, I greeted the farmers from the terrace. They had been arranging lovely flower beds on the ground, and they took off their coppola caps, fell to their knees, prostrate, with Sasà Siniscalchi who bid them remain in their underwear in the presence of that saint, who, from the azure of the terrace, was forgiving them for nothing more than living on 500 lira a day.

During the breaks, Lydia was adored in the church. I was on horseback dressed in Renaissance armor astride a mare that risked a generous gallop. Lydia, still wearing her halo, would drive the white car, dangerously distracting & threatening the lives of truck drivers and delivery van drivers, who would brake abruptly and look back at her to see if it hadn't been some sort of hallucination.

In fact, Lydia-Madonna was transporting an empty car while munching on a huge sandwich. Masini was all curled up in a ball in the slightly ajar trunk, and behind Masini was a knight — that would be me — a knight from other times riding his horse and holding in his arms a dying young girl in pink garments whose breasts were exposed to the wind.

There were plenty of things to drive them crazy, those primitive folks, who were not at all accustomed to the world of cinema.

At night, when we were lucky, the heroic Masini and I would get three hours of sleep. But more often than not, we didn't get more than a half hour, particularly when I had to prepare the next day's *décor* myself, which sometimes meant adorning the Moorish villa's many cupolas with flags and banners.

These and an infinite number of other stressful circumstances comprised what *Our Lady of the Turks* was in the year '68 — an expressly anti-'68 film, in contempt not only of that "Italian-Gallic May," but also of all the socio-elite "Mays" in History in sæcula sæculorum.

"THOSE WHO SEE, DON'T SEE WHAT THEY SEE..."

We filmed the last sequences in a deconsecrated church, rural and Pascolian, but very beautiful because of the shattered Baroque stone angels that had been painted pink. During the breaks, Madonna-Lydia, sitting on a pew and smoking a cigarette, would implore me, while I, atop my horse, would let in the plebs because they insisted on kissing the hem of the Holy Mother's dress, oblivious to the fact that she was half-dressed, smoking, and reading *Annabella*.

"You're so beautiful!... You're so beautiful!" The only thing I could do, out of breath from trying to get a recalcitrant horse to climb up the altar, was to elicit the help of the cops to quell those mystical tumults.

The film was presented at that year's Venice film festival. Luigi Chiarini, the last priest worthy of the altars destined for the "uncouth splendor," issued a press release stating that my debut film was more than enough to represent Italy. In any event, the Venice festival was swept away that year by all kinds of mutinies by authors uniformly wardrobed in the euphoria of the current trends.

It was the last "golden" year of the "lions."

I took the silver lion. Oh well. I couldn't have expected anything more. Otherwise, they would have arrested the Japanese members of the jury, Doniol-Valcroze, Chiarini, and the others. An ambulance would have arrived by sea to intervene.

As soon as it was certain that my film would be representing Italy, 10 other Italians came out of the woodwork: Bertolucci, Cavani, Pasolini, Risi, etc. Not a single one of them would take away an award. I, on the other hand, received in recompense a distribution-punishment in the "sacred" circuit of the *cinéma d'essai*.

During the screening at the Excelsior, everything imaginable occurred: tumults, applause, slaps in the face for Mazzarella di Perla Peragallo, etc. So, friends surrounded me, like Mario Ricci, Leo De Berardinis, Piero Panza, Cosimo Cinieri, who stood by me through the whole thing, including the indiscreet surveillance of 40, unfortunately not so undercover, policemen meant to keep an eye on me and prevent me from getting up to no good.

The situation was reversed three years later, in '71, when I was back in Venezia with *Salome*, and 40 policemen were mobilized to protect me.

Our Lady of the Turks was a cry for the new cinema that had been born. But in Italy, it only takes turning your back for a moment, and you no longer exist. You never did.

Another caprice followed this caprice: *Capricci*. My second ruinous film. Ruinous in every sense. Including financially.

Capricci was a *mélange* of *Arden of Feversham* and a version of *Manon* that I had conceived of years earlier.

Alongside Anne Wiazemsky, still sprightly, venerable old men, like Davoli, Gulà, etc., who were open to anything *&* everything, acted in the film.

Here, too, the whole thing was a rather savory, but also ostentatious, theatrical parody of the image. A film poorly shot intentionally. A lot of imbeciles, so many critics, at the Cannes Festival's "Quinzaine des réalisateurs," where the film was presented, even though dedicating entire pages to it and praising it as my best work (clearly, they had already forgotten about *Our Lady of the Turks*), did their best to obfuscate my candid film and to disfigure it with their "interpretations." Noting that the protagonist used a car (as a weapon) to commit suicide, they interpreted cars to mean consumer society, and so a film that referenced Godard's *Week End*, etc.

Nothing could have been further from the truth. It was merely one way, among many, to commit suicide. I chose to use a car instead of a knife for the simple reason that it was more ostentatious, a metal sheet instead of a metal blade, like a blow-up, an exaggeration of a pocket knife, of a razor.

The critics were capable of making this blunder and didn't seem to want to notice the most important thing — the only thing that was meant to remain in the film's *bricolage* — that is, this ensemble of the half-naked Susanne and the old men who, during the breaks from the set in Tonino Caputi's house, would sleep, all piled up, half-naked, one on top of another on furs ridden with fleas that were acquired in via Sannio. Young women in the best of health and decrepit old men about to have heart attacks from the temptation of seeing so much rosy flesh. In fact, nearly all of the latter were dead not long after that.

We wanted to demean every temptation of Art with that parade of decrepit old debris coagulated in actors and crucifixes. *Capricci* was not understood. The so-called critical attention it received was derailed by the car debacle.

The parody of "creation" by images in the destruction of all that the painter was creating was misunderstood. The painter in *Arden of Feversham* is he who poisons with his paintings, who intoxicates with images. The repugnance for the image went further and further defining itself in language, cartoonishly parodied and dissipated on the path to the *phoné*.

Everything in life takes place between old men. Antiquity is *old*. All the passions are old. So much old age in that film!

The production manager called them for dubbing (extremely arbitrary dubbing because it was done without the visuals and only later "synchronized" by the "lifer" Contini, who, in the editing room, had them saying things they had never said, or things they had said in other "parts" of the film). Some of the old men asked on the phone how they should dress for the dubbing. Others, who hadn't even thought to ask, appeared wearing clothes as if on the set, heavy capes, hats, and tattered umbrellas.

Speaking of tattered umbrellas… It was raining yesterday at the Versiliana Festival. Ruggero Orlando, one of my dearest friends, was presenting his *Delta del Po*, & I couldn't miss it. At the end, he asked me to stand next to him, and at that moment Edmonda Aldini, who had been asked to greet the audience, emerged from the jumble & couldn't stop herself from saying to me, "…The microphone always makes the voice beautiful…" The usual nonsense spouted by theater people, who are condemned to misunderstand that which is word and that which is *phoné*, voice.

When *Don Giovanni* came out in 1971, Callisto Cosulich wrote an apologia in the *ABC* of the time, calling it "Our Eisenstein of the bedroom. A splendid work that alone justifies the arrival of videocassettes."

Don Giovanni, based on Barbey d'Aurevilly's novella, my third heroic cinematographic adventure, was filmed on a set the size of a broom closet.

The film ends with the camera entering the emptiness of an immense frame that fades to black, while a quote from Borges in English runs across the screen: *Mirrors and copulation are abominable, since they both multiply the numbers of men.*

Everything in the film proclaimed the impossibility of a masculine dongiovannism. In that wide variety of exhibited nudes, of female faces made-up to appear different, it was always the same nude, always the same woman's face.

In the same face, in the same woman, always the same lack of interest from Don Giovanni, subtracted from the pitiful variety "of every shape, of every age," and ruinously drawn toward the deceptive sex that was still a little girl who had not withered into a woman.

In any event, what *Don Giovanni* shows is an indifference for the list.

Everything in the film was rigorously predetermined to avoid any ambiguity with respect to dongiovannism. Lydia's own nude scenes variously reproduced poses from Rembrandt, details from Botticelli's *Primavera*, from Ingres's *Baigneuse*, from Titian, from Velázquez, etc., etc., and then, little by little, cropped by the camera itself.

The only thing that remains of the list is numeration, and of the numeration, the number one dressed in women's make-up, and therefore made-up with nothing.

Make-up that the more that it allows itself to be seen, the more it attracts in its vertiginous number. Vertigo of numbers. A bliss better suited to a mathematician than to an amateur.

Woman. We can only but *count her* in Leporello and *never find her* in Don Giovanni. It is in this never finding her that Don Giovanni "womanizes himself."

That which comes back here like clockwork between the scent of woman and rumpled sheets is always the impossibility of *coucher avec*. A thousand and three missed opportunities.

... Accused of "impotence" by scholars with a feminist bent, celebrated, rather, by Da Ponte as a champion of masculine power, I believe that the time has come to restore Don Giovanni to the femininity that is truly his own — robbed a thousand and three times, he took it back a thousand and three times.

The body of every undressed woman is an irreducible land, a limit that excludes every conquest. "Conquest" in Don Giovanni is his very own loss every time, in that swooning that destroys the illusion of any sex and any relationship between the sexes. Don Giovanni a conqueror, yes, but of his own defeat. "Crazy" from a thousand and three misadventures, the seducer cannot but end up in the ruin that germinates in him and that overflows into the *feminine*.

The womanizer par excellence will never again find woman in the body of a woman. It was fatal for him to have diverted his gaze for a moment. Exceeded desire reveals itself from so much obscenity.

So much so that in a future *mise en scène* of *Don Juan*, in order to say everything there is to say about the impossibility of a connection between the sexes, I would abandon Donn'Anna and all the Donn'Annas on earth to burn with desire, naked *&* alone on stage, leaving Don Giovanni the pleasure of masturbating elsewhere.

A truly grandiose performance of weakness.

It is impossible to access *Don Giovanni* if not by dodging the circuits of eroticism.

If Don Giovanni is what I think he is.

To read Don Giovanni as a "transgressor of laws" is another temptation that is all too obvious. Since it says nothing of his empty beds, of the defeat of his nights.

Everything is suspended in a frigid repetition of acts, in a necessity that does not allow passion and always returns there, where emptiness is made.

When he makes his own woman of himself.

His night of love is a description of a battle forever lost. With absolutely no way out, just as Kierkegaard had partially understood. Whatever the manner in which we speak, and here we are speaking about "love," we nevertheless arrive at the *suspension of the tragic*, which, in dongiovannism, becomes pornomania as soon as the truth is revealed. A deranged state of grace in which the *comic* is supplanted by the *ridiculous*, when even the bodies are reduced to the pure number of an infinite deferment.

People wanted to make *Don Giovanni* a "game of intercourse" but instead it is a game that suspends and erases any sort of intercourse, where the rule is that the *coucher* takes place in one room and the *avec* in another. Properly dislocated in the discourse, the bodies can even lie in the same bed.

I had to unscrew the myth from the shameful cross of sex. Me, I was Don Giovanni. I was him in those rumpled beds, in the wanton sweat of bodies. I was more *&* more him in the need that came less *&* less often, in the desire that abandoned me.

A Commendatore comes to reprimand him unnecessarily. Don Giovanni returns from his own private hell on his own. He has left hell. He has become his own Lazarus, "come back to tell you everything." *Don Giovanni* eschews interpretation. It is the "interpretive key" tossed in the sea.

I cannot think of Don Giovanni without feeling like Don Kappa, a dreadful pornographer who nips any bud of poetry as soon as it sprouts, or any smile from a "beautiful soul."

Two different rooms, or, even better, two different centuries; only then is the paradox of copulation possible.

EDUARDO

I've known Eduardo for more than 15 years. He used to come to listen to me, even in the basement theater. I remember him perched like a raven on one of the many school desks. Afterwards, we would get together with Elsa Morante on one terrace or another and talk about theater, literature, and often about music. He would ask me, "So, have you made any money in theater?" "No," I would say, "I haven't made any money yet. I don't think anyone can make money in theater." "That's too bad. It means you're an idiot."

That's what we talked about on Elsa's terrace so many, so very many, years ago. Eduardo was right. Back then, I was a poor idiot. Now, I'm a wealthy idiot, and that suits me just fine.

But getting back to Eduardo and me together on stage, I want to remember exactly what it was about Eduardo that no one ever understood.

They say of Eduardo: "His comedies published in Einaudi's 'Millennium Collection' of the dead do not measure up to the Eduardo on stage, who at times is sublime, etc..." Here, it needs to made clear that Eduardo attends to the smallest of details even in the other actors' performances. He rehearses over and over again those so-called improvisations "a soggetto" until he collapses, until the actors pass out, until he himself passes out. He is hard on himself and hard on others, because he knows very well that everything, even the smallest of details, has to function properly, so that nothing is missing on stage.

That meticulousness is what is so particular about his mise-en-scènes.

Of course, being the great actor that he is, Eduardo writes something "beforehand" that he can later undermine when on stage. I'm not sure how aware of it he is, but he readies his own trap, the notorious play that he really believes he will leave to posterity. In this, he is Quixotic, and I love him for it. How can anyone not love *Don Quixote*?

In the act of writing, he anticipates how he will later manage this material, which will in fact be contradicted on stage, where even a single sentence can occupy an hour and a half. He gains in the moment a written scene that, on the one hand, has nothing to do with what we consider dramatic writing "beforehand," and that, on the other hand, would be impossible to accomplish without the handicap of a pre-writing.

I remember one time when I, Vittorio Gassman, and Eduardo were invited to be interviewed by Nicola Chiaromonte from *L'Espresso*, since we were the most "important" examples of three different generations in Italian theater. He wanted to use the occasion to stir up polemics between us on our visions of theater, but the more we talked about it, the more we found that we were extraordinarily of the same mind.

When a bit later Chiaromonte asked Eduardo, "What can we do for the actor?" He replied, "Complicate his life."

Precisely. Eduardo is a master of continually preparing impediments and traps for himself on stage. His much-vaunted dramaturgy is nothing other than this enormous trap that makes rehearsals a means of disentangling yourself, of escaping from them.

I think that this Hölderlinian dissonance in Eduardo finds its concordance precisely in the schizophrenia between the pre-written text and the stage text.

This, it must be said, only works for Eduardo. Nor should the other playwrights delude themselves by entrusting their pieces to others. Eduardo tried it anyway, by entrusting his pieces to Laurence Olivier, with disastrous results.

With respect to Eduardo's "charisma," I can say that it comes from his exceptional professionalism, a professionalism I have never encountered in anyone else. I remember at the Teatro Verdi in Pisa (there too, the theater was packed with healthy euphoria), at the end of the performance, Eduardo wanted to speak from the proscenium, foregoing the use of the microphone we had set up for him. The audience, which had grown accustomed to listening to amplified voices, could not hear him. Somebody yelled out, "Sound!"

He was devilish and flippant, "... Eh, eh... excuse me, I was actually talking about things that are none of your business."

But as soon as we had left the theater — because there was an "encore" between rounds of applause — he says to me, "You see, I stopped smoking for this. That man was right. Why don't you stop too?"

Then the next day: a reception in our honor at Pisa's city hall. Between an award & a recognition, a woman, the regional assessor, penetrated the mayor's office. She addressed me first, "Ah, so you're Carmelo Bene. It's a shame that you mistreat women like you do..."

"... Not at all. You're mistaken about me. I do not mistreat women... I wish there was one..."

Ill at ease, the assessor sought refuge on the couch next to Eduardo, confident in finding herself in better company.

In his eternal good "bad faith," Eduardo attempted to comfort her, by telling her something about his marriages.

"I once had a wife, who, at a certain point was called to meet her maker. I would write all the time, even at night, and I would smoke a lot, I would smoke and write. So, I got worried, because when she was alive she was always threatening me, 'You write only because I exist. If I were to cease to exist, you wouldn't be able to write another word...'" Eduardo went on, "So, when she died, I abstained from picking up a pen for seven or eight months, because she had thoroughly convinced me that, without her as my Muse, I wouldn't be able to write."

At the moment when the assessor was at the height of joy for what seemed to be the greatest of tributes to women, Eduardo went on to say, "... But toward the eighth or ninth month, I attempted, with trepidation, to pick up a pen, and I realized that I could still write without... (her)."

The assessor's face began to change color when Eduardo's second story definitively (dis)comforted her:

"... Then there was my second wife, and the same thing happened with her, the same misfortune... a few months of abstinence from the pen & then I still wrote without... (her), until I found Isabella."

"Whereas the first two wives were not writers, and knew nothing about literature and poetry, Isabella was well-read, and she was even a writer herself. Such that, from the moment we met we were on the same page: 'What do you do, do you write?' 'Yes!' 'So, let's do this; let's compare our poems, and we'll see which ones are the best...' For her, my poems were the best ones, so she tore up her own poems and threw them in the trash, and from that moment on she decided to take care of me and nurse me — Laforgue would have said — 'a nurse for the love of art.'"

The look on the assessor's face when she heard that was indescribable.

Let's just say that she vanished.

PARODIES

If heroism has (is) a laugh, then the Borgesian game of intentional anachronism and erroneous attribution reflects it as the *very same's* greatest derision. I have said elsewhere that *parody* and *tragedy* are one and the same thing, but in the same bosom. Therefore, we reassure the spectator's voyeuristic anti-heroism in theater always in two acts: a first act assigned to the fruition of the socio-adversarial "tragedy"; and a second act, which takes place in another theater entirely, to the amateur actors' "enjoyment" (at its best: an Italian para-political cabaret) to serve as the lighthearted parody of that "tragic" act that preceded it. It is precisely this way of dividing into two acts the "dark" entertainment intended by the audience to stage games to synthesize the beggarly cowardice that resides in all spectators.

With respect to the critics on the early Carmelo Bene, I still think of Flaiano, "This country of ours is a country in which nothing is taken seriously, but woe betide he who seems like he wants to joke around." It's an inhospitable land for certain kinds of acrobats "with their feet firmly planted in the clouds."

In the *"republic of the public square"* (Flaiano again) — as is indicated on the pavement markings — there has always been a place where people grow bored of crying, and another where they laugh from boredom.

Collective boredom is a *privilege of membership*, a constant of participation, in theater and in life, in other people's misfortunes.

Ultimately, all these good people who, buried in the electoral ballot boxes, and nothing more than witnesses to soccer games, feel like they have finally heard the clamorous call of their country; inasmuch as these good people are "history," they laugh, assassins of their very own grief, which they do not recognize as their own, since schizophrenia and consumption allow them to see as *separate* what for the poet is all at once "disconnectedly visible for two" in its production.

Let's cut to the chase. If the "tragic" in theater is an absurd routine, because deprived of parody (which it sometimes includes involuntarily), then "parody" is artificial, displaced, parroted, allusive and impervious to serendipity — unless a "comic actor" collapses on the floor from a heart attack — it is always a revolting and vulgar performance; and the consensuses it reaps are the yardsticks that measure (for whoever is still interested) the public anti-heroism that knows how to laugh at this and at that, but never at itself. This audience, in turn, always finds those "part" actors on stage, that bestiary of "kiss-asses" and "fart-sniffers" as a mirror, — either this or that; out of role, outside of "role playing," no one.

Unearthing a little piece of anachronism, here is Goffredo Fofi in *Quaderni Piacentini* observing, and how!, that *The Last Tango in Paris* is a miserable parody of that *Last Tango in Zagarolo*, which was legitimately elected as the "original." Just like Paolo Poli's stagings of *La Nemica* and *Rita da Cascia* are poor simulacra of the prototypes superbly revisited by the "D'Origlia-Palmi company."

"EUSEBIO"

1982. The 50th anniversary of Dino Campana's death.

We'll celebrate the author of the *Orphic Songs* in the middle of our next theatrical misery, and we'll move people with the requisite incomprehension.

Last night, a lady — certainly not "Our" lady — with a degree in numbers and in the muses of physics, having little to no intellect for written verse, expressed her admiration for Montale's postcard poetry. The lady feigned to seek other opinions, since, having seen the poet with her own eyes in another time, and having fallen in love with him, though it was unclear why, she resolutely would not relent — it's understandable — about the importance of her having "seen the poet," & she went on to defend "Eusebio's" verses, though no attack had been launched against them, though, indeed, those verses lack poetry.

Eliot, Pound, Laforgue. What can I say? Gozzano. She was brilliantly unaware of all those masters who wove the wind of "the accident" Montale.

That's enough, Madam. Let's call to mind these few verses that will be sufficient to demonstrate that this Eusebio of ours had a deep aversion for the inconveniences associated with writing poetry:

> *think* my soul (not so beautiful), no longer divided:
> to change the elegy into a hymn, *to reinvent myself,*
> *to no longer be missed…*

"Beautiful" soul, evoked (referred to). To what? To thinking. Thinking about what? About reinventing the self (the comfort of being). "To no longer be missed" (and is poetry not its own lack?). Is it not rather a loan shark's will? Tight-fisted Montale. His is an attempt at poetry to occupy his spare time. The verses, the sounds, with a few exceptions, are decidedly not essential for him. And he knew it. But if others were pleased…

> Today, we can tell you only this,
> That which we are *not*, that which we do *not* want.

We might have hoped that this insolent (word for word) citation from Nietzsche's *The Gay Science* would have horrified him of the prospect of the eternal return.

Italian literary critics' opinions are not that far off from those of that misguided lady from last night.

As for me, I spent time with this "Eusebio," for the sake of my friends, over the course of more than 15 summers in Versilia, unfortunately, both for him and for me. He used to call me Malvolio, and I was at the time — him, he would sleep — a sultan, a ladies' man.

On certain afternoons, in the painter Nino Tirinnanzi's arbors, the poet of seaside discontents would stain rather expensive drawing paper with coffee dregs, with orange soda, and other messes (a clumsy abuse of one system among many of Rosai's pupil), and myself along with Tirinnanzi and Bodini — the unforgettable Vittorio — were submitted to forced judgments on those unpoetic watercolors, which we ruthlessly rejected (comparing those little visual games to his poetry). Montale, grumbling silently, whistled little baritone arias to the skies, inured by then to our —solicited — rude teasing.

Then there was another time, when Henry-sculptor-Moore was talking to me — in improvised Esperanto — about color temperatures. A big couch. Montale happened to be on my right, and the Bodini-demon was sitting next to him.

Our "Eusebio" inopportunely passed one watercolor after another to me, so that I could give them to Moore to look at. I gave them to him, saying nothing about the author, and Moore didn't know it was Montale. It quickly became an amusing, infantile competition to bombard the suffocating logs in the fireplace with the balled-up messages from the poet who had turned into a stony Don Pasquale. Moore was having the time of his life. He would pretend to study the drawings from right to left, and then upside down; then his face lit up, and he winked at me as he invited me to watch a basketball game in the living room.

So, dear lady, the Ungaretti-Quasimodo-Montales of this world, an earthly limbo of bullishness, are not then all that innocent, no, not really.

On Marinetti, we might be so bold as to say, "He's a dimwit with flashes of imbecility." That sounds about right.

On the abuses & miseries of these others, aside from late night gossip, "it's better not to talk about life here."

Poetry is detachment, distance, absence, separation, illness, delirium, sound, and, above all, urgency, life, suffering (not necessarily the Christian kind). It is the ebb and flow of the intolerance of the being there. It is discontent, even in the "happiest" of cases. It is the saying's resonance beyond the concept. It is a musical interval at its greatest heights, lyric, in which we say the disillusion expressed by that other interval (distance) between the "conceit" and its record on the page. It is the abyss that differentiates the oral from the written.

As for the dregs at the bottom of the coffee cup, well, there is Pasternak for that; yes, him, the singer of cosmic trifles.

Goodbye good lady: a "rotten" poet (Alberto Moravia says a rotten "to the core" poet filled with fervor) is not always a premise that guarantees a good poet. So, to you who were hesitating on the threshold, at four o'clock in the morning, holding your umpteenth glass of wine in your hand, uncertain if you should put down that object and disappear, or if you should stay where you are, and send home the wine:

"EUSEBIO"

"You see, my dear, perhaps, who knows, one day, you will be able to tell the story of having met me, of having talked with me. But what story would I tell, what story?"

FROM POETRY TO THEATER

"The poet of the stage," that's what they call me. And yet, mean-spirited, lurking there a hint of the pejorative, a little like in the games played on stage, "poet" might sound diminutive next to the actor's *grandeur*. So, is it a backhanded compliment? It would seem so; but let's have a little fun *&* follow this gluttonous byzantinism for a while. Always on stage:

Is the actor-poet, therefore, a thespian who is less talented than the thespian; and is the latter less a poet than the former?

Is poetry a dramatic deficiency and vice-versa? Let's take this slowly. So: theatricality at its apex is unpoetic; it is not by chance that it is insulted as condescending prose and is happy for it. The "poetical," for its part, is unworthy, unsuitable for theater. Ah, ah, ah, let's turn this argument around and change direction to start with another point of departure, from the moment that so-called actors take the stage and dare to perform in verse their fettered and unfettered Œdipuses, Electras, Antigones *&* Prometheuses. Here, too, the actor-poet scale weighs none of it with any accuracy.

Let's stick to poetry so we will understand each other.

Contemporary "Imagisms" aside, the cynic Zeno says in a fragment, *"The voice is the dialectic of thought."*

You see, what a Macedonian coup. I have no interest in descriptive verse, little exercises in landscapes, verse, in short, as composition, seeing as how it is the equivalent of the unfortunate parroting of every single actor I know of on stage. And in that sense, the universal "classical" tradition is an infinite cemetery of actor-poets and poet-actors. But if poeticizing beyond "emotions" is the *exercise* in an *entirely different* language that rigorously prevents every *extra-textual* temptation, then here we find the sound's supreme game (abandonment) inasmuch as it is a text of saying that the voice *writes* in the middle of the exchanges on stage.

We do not call anyone an actor who does not go beyond recounting another saying that he writes. He un-writes.

So, *actor* and *poet* are *one and the same*.

In composite "poetry," a "poet" may not be an actor, just like in a composite theater, an "actor" may not be a poet.

But we have acknowledged the "composition" as entirely foreign to the poetry of saying. So, the *poet* is necessarily an *actor*, like Jekyll is Hyde (his hiding from himself) and not one or the other disguised in turns. *He who is not a poet is not an actor on stage.*

If the contentious and nonsensical guerilla warfare between the poets and the "poets" who lack voice continues, then all the bickering in the theater dissipates.

It is not by chance that, among the many misunderstandings there are in theater, poetry (representation) is considered an (in)considerate maidservant to "prose" on stage.

Someone will remind me that there is an *essence* of the poet in each and every one of us on earth; very well, but a "poet" of the image made plain. A poet of writing as saying, no, not that one. Not unless we consider mundane rumors poetry as well.

We need urgency — to not be in the sounds to give voice to forgotten thought.

We need a somewhat unhappy apprenticeship, *&* then *a beyond* happy unhappiness.

"ROMEO AND JULIET" IN PARIS

Under the star of Maria Callas, my performances at the Opéra Comique received enthusiastic acclaim. Bel Canto, the café-bar neighboring the artists' entrance. Here, in the early evening, while waiting to conquer those refined Gauls, Saint-Pierre Klossowski the polytheist and I were celebrating. A religious concoction of vodka and kir.

"You do realize, Pierre, that I have to perform in about an hour." But that didn't bother that Knight Templar of transgression's unwavering, steadfast, intoxicated faith. Between one offertory and another, in a mere "breath," he was polishing off his duties for the Holy See without a care, so as to happily return to my voice in terrible French. You see, we were talking idly about the recent news regarding the old God's dead body that was never found; about His anything but divine incomprehension of the celestial others, from the moment that he got the truly terrible idea in his head to consider himself the "one *&* only."

Knight Templar-Saint Pierre, in his impeccable Ecclesiastical Latin, always thirsty for the in no way Christian-blood-kir, poorly concealed with an angelic smile a certain vague misgiving of his with respect to the current *&* future fates of the Antichrist.

"*Vous comprenez, cher Carmelo,*" and he pulled me aside, wine glass in hand, in an anachronistic search for a little corner as if at the Council of Trent; and then briefly, innocent and circumspect, in his academic Latin, inspired, he lamented the, at this point, shameless absence of the Crucified Christ in laic scholars' works on the eternal return.

"How is it possible?" He was mortified for these scholars. "There cannot be an Antichrist if there is no Christ." Nietzschean heresy persisted, in other words, in an inadmissible dogma not only in the eyes of His Holiness the Pope, but also in the eyes of any discerning, wandering cleric.

A theater apprentice cut through the crowd of devotees in the Bel Canto sacristy to remind me that my turn to preach to the laypeople was coming up within the next half hour. I was forced to leave the *Gran Maestro*, however, well before he arrived at the Agnus Dei in the mass he was saying. We were to meet the next day, at the same time, in that secret audience; but there was a hiccup, so he planned to put off one of his intrigues with the Holy See so we could meet.

The velvet curtain opened, and I found myself once again being poured from a gigantic crystalline chalice onto the wine-colored carpet on stage, sheltered by a sky clothed in enormous, purple silk roses.

"Have no faith in me, workers. Having no faith consoles, guides, and heals. Do not pray for me, I command you. I ask only for your lack of faith, so that I can die happy."

The usual half hour of "triumph," & then, in the dressing room, the unusual visitation from Jacques Lacan.

"*Bonsoir, maître.*"

"*Jacques Lacan, pas maître.*"

The maestro was dressed in midnight blue, and he was accompanied by Madame Nobecourt. A crowd of solicitous souls had been kept from entering the *loge*. And what did those photojournalists have their minds set on? Documenting the Parisian elite comprised of the two of us, ectoplasms of nomination?

"O how mundane it all is." The futility of meeting in the imaginary of the eyes. David Harali's comatose photos — where the dead-not dead were still agitated and focused on their attempt to remain immobile in the carefully prepared trench graves — were peeking at me from the make-up table.

Had Lacan not heard the Klossowskian breaths from that *Romeo and Juliet*? Had the overplayed representation of bodies "separated" from their "souls" extraordinarily escaped his notice?

Dripping with sweat, facing him, statuesque, I closed my eyes & I heard his voice, "I want to reread all of Shakespeare." Once again, a prophet, I turned my back to him so that I might see him facing me in the mirror. His hair was silver.

At that moment, I did not realize that this reciprocal silence in behavioral suspicion was a respite from acting-suffering. I thought back on my eternally-returning Saint-Pierre and how infantile he is, like me; to the rhizomatic energy, yes, the agile super-intelligence of Gilles Deleuze, to our — *coup de foudre* — solidified friendship, to that generosity of thought that we don't give each other, how we fall in love, when necessary. Whereas he, the blue-silvered Jacques Lacan, whom I resembled by innate destiny, he remained silent. I remained silent. It's true that in theology we are meant to listen; replies are not permitted. But two people who are both listening? Yes, ok, but what then? Was it listening that was listening? Absolutely.

Were we avoiding mundane small talk, little courtesies? Of course, we were; there was nothing else. The idiotic followers of "Lacanianism," who had been refused entry here, were spying on us through closed windows over there at the neighboring Bel Canto café. The pathetic, arrogant, voiceless paper hereditariness. You can be poor, and, oh well, you deal with it. But to be poor and "Lacanian" is a catastrophe: this same fairy tale rewritten by several idiots, what "does it mean," it doesn't mean a damn thing.

There in the mirror, I glimpsed the unwieldy emptiness vainly filling the seminars in the disciple Lacan's eyes. Faith's foolishness in finding "its own" language among the countless student-teachers; those curious students that only Paris knows how "to educate" early in things that are inasmuch as they are not.

At this point, my tired gaze doubled, and I saw two Saint Theresas of the orgasm. One, who had been raved about at the castle of the Knights Templar, was equipped with a phallus and breasts heavy with milk. The other was unaware of her Lacanian-God-*Jouissance*. Androgynous knowledge of milk and sperm, and the abandonment of Berninian ecstasy, her unhappy ignorant absence.

Then, yet another, a third Theresa who kept watch over the silence of C.B. *&* J.L., and who may have been reading the initial "T" that starts her name among the stars in the sky.

Nothing remained speechless between the mirrors in that dressing room.

Romeo was still lamenting his death, shipwrecked between Gustav Mahler's notes. And the incantation of saying was still suspended between the "breaths," comforted by our polite refusal of having anything to add.

In my lucid exhaustion, Lacan's superintelligence deserved this unforgotten, empty encounter, conceding nothing at all in terms of a phrastic occasion for those courtesies that human beings steal from one another *daily* in misunderstandings disguised as "relationships."

Lacan, or the suspension of dialogue. This, my friends, is what "reciprocal" esteem means; far from false and true modesty.

Yes, this is what it means *to miss*. In this sense, certain of Aleksandr Blok's verses, which would otherwise be obscure, sound evangelical to me:

> Since what is better in this world
> if not to lose best friends.

Oh, if only we encountered our "true love" at one time or another, we would know in that moment how much *we were* missing. But to meet real absence is an extraordinary, horrible consolation. It makes us masterpieces of anxiety beyond ourselves. And masterpieces don't give a damn about art.

Lacan discreetly disappeared in the midst of the photographers' flashes. I'm aware that, prompted by profane gossip surrounding the event, he dealt with the frivolous snooping of the reporters, who had been condemned to exact a quote from him on my theatrical being, "*Dans tous les cas il sait ce qu'il fait,*" he said and thundered off, like a receding storm.

Gilles Deleuze. What a nice surprise, in the cellar bar of the cloister hotel after the performance. Deleuze is a self-destroyer. He, this human *computer*, smokes too much, and he ought not to in his condition. He reads as much as he writes, and vice-versa. Gilles is *the* surprise. In most people, and in the best of cases, somewhat talented work comes from eclectic learning, whereas in him, it comes from extraordinary unlearning. With Gilles it is never the occasion for a fixed meeting. It is the becoming in its occasions. It could seem like outdated bickering to whoever may have pigeonholed (and harm was done, if that someone actually did it) Deleuze into libertine thought, etc. He is not that at all. Why should I even care about proving it to you? Am I backing Deleuze? I'm saying this to myself, letting myself say it. Dammit, dammit to the bookshelves! To the devil (if he's available) with the obese fear of a specialism in wavering doubt; of this or that "excess." Well, yes, we are asphyxiated from thoughtless, antiheroic, poetic and unpoetic "pondering," and therefore malodorous, up to our ears in the beggarly exclusivism of author's rights; asphyxiated from the ostentatious superiority deceived in "the same" of the work displayed once and for all; from the lyricism of life-long senators. Let's end this once and for all, with this constipation of the *de-generate* (genre), with this uncivilized absconding. Political poetry no longer exists; and whereas Alberto Savinio longed for it (a luxury of livable small cities and towns), it is futile at this point to grieve for it.

Gilles is unavailable. He's everywhere. I believe him to be the greatest thinking machine in the drought of our times. He is all-absorbed, and, if he falls in love with a *quid*, it's said, it's written, and it costs him nothing. He is the *excess*. And the "excess" "is in between, or it's the middle (*milieu*)."

Yes, indeed, the philosopher, the author of *Difference and Repetition* is *naturaliter* the lucid connoisseur (Deleuze, that is) of theater, of music, of any *&* every kind of sport, of cinema, flamenco, tap dance, of the anachronistic *fado*, of the *phoné*, of drops in the sea.

And when the adorable Jean-Paul Manganaro made it known that *Le Monde* wanted him to write a full-page portrait of Carmelo Bene (toasting to the emptiness of happiness, I had gotten myself all worked up to tell him about a project of mine on *Richard III*, where the actor would be the sum of deformed artificial limbs against obscene history), he said, "I'll write a book! Who cares about newspapers!"

Gilles never ceases to amaze me. And write it he did, without even seeing the play. He wrote *me*. Then I wrote the text that he would see in my last Roman play at the Teatro Quirino four months after the publication of his book. And at the end of the play, in the dressing room, he embraced me and sat down wearily in the chair, with eyes full of enthusiasm, as expected:

"*Oui, oui, c'est la rigueur.*"

That's it. You think it's not enough? After this swift little story, do you feel like revisiting the "methodology" of our experts in critical literary, theatrical, and musical studies and so on & so forth? No, that would be ungrateful. If anything, it's upsetting that these bewildered scribes, that these far too many distractions from "God's handiwork" inhabit our world and, what is worse, that they are convinced of being there, miserable wretches abandoned for good from abandonment; in this respect, similar to the squalid circumstances of "happy" poets.

Oh, here's a good one, & I nearly forgot to tell it. At my Parisian "premieres" the indignation of the critics from the special drama gazettes spread openly when spotting some "intruders" in the theater (Deleuze, Lacan, Klossowski, Foucault, and others "like them").

"Time is out of joint, now even thinkers go to the theater!"

Then two years later, on the occasion of my "premiere" of the *Manfred*-Byron-Schumann at the Scala, where, while the audience was revering, the theater and music critics were babbling, disoriented between the grade-scale of the "singing recitation" and other stupidities; here you are again, Deleuze, come to the rescue to enthusiastically explain C.B.'s proposition, not as a phenomenon of "greatness," but rather as a confrontation and subsequent victory of "the mode" (and, well, it just so happens that in the old days people used to call "affects" musical "modes") precisely where *"the affects become modes."*

Repetition is difference without a concept. He who is absorbed in this does not know what to do with paltry conflictual theater.

But those many who are invested with the "charge of…," to whom vertigo is precluded, delude themselves in recounting theatrical stories to their neighbor, the painless misdeeds of mnemonic simulation of the "scripts" from the gallows-amateur actor boards of the "I" who, with a text written beforehand, informed them in turn of what they already "knew." ("What matters — is the routine actress following her method — is that they (don't) know that we know that they know.")

Would you like an example of an irreversible opposite? Of course:

I (the C.B. of the theater) *am what I lack.* It is a nonexistent theater that is tired of the being there. It is eternal de-dramatization as dismantling.

This I of mine is both Cleopatra and Anthony together.

Getting back to the daily press, how, for God's sake, can they report this lack? They can't, so what are the poor things after? It's blatantly obvious:

C.B. is something entirely other. *From the remainder and not himself.*

The alienation-*quotidie* grocery shopping-home-paycheck-rent slips and falls on its ever "decorous" ass; and it is from such great heights that we arrive at deranged enunciations: "Hamlet-Shakespeare, the integral edition" (disintegrated in Italian, just like how Dante's *"Au milieu du chemin de la vie"* sounds in French and so on in silence). The "development of the character," deplorable "interpretation" is everywhere (how lucky they are with their stable identities to dress themselves in "other's clothes").

C.B. is *different* only in the *same*. The Will he's left with is the ruin of the nothingness in which he consists. His plan to un-memorize is the impossible vacation in Colonus. Because C.B. can only do what he cannot. He can only do the impossible.

And you architects of dreams (satisfied desires), to hear you half-wits talk about it, you who are proud of being there; to hear you talk about it, C.B. is a separate chapter on how to make theater. But you should know that C.B. is prepared to definitively defile the borrowed brain you praise by annihilating himself in *Macbeth* '82-83. You'll go home after the show of restless nothingness, rubbing yourselves against your lady repression; you'll scribble *more solito* your "piece," about the unusual nature of the unspeakable event. C.B. will be a poet, but interdicted from your abandoned railroad. C.B. is the process of his own regression. Until lifeless.

Life, however ugly or beautiful you like, is yours; a rag that's not half bad from your local flea market whose tickle makes you feel alive. Nothingness rejects you.

C.B. looks into the void. And, in him, "Bibi" Shakespeare is a certain smile belonging to things that are not.

Foucault (another Simonist "intruder," who, like a thief, penetrated the mysteries of the Opéra Comique to the indignation of the priesthood's "expert") understands — he is another one who is absorbed — without having to rack his brains, the blinding, derisory servant-master parody staged by C.B. to the sacrosanct detriment of the Marxist "Hommelette," which was greeted by a thunderous ovation at its "premiere" in French, as it is spoken in Marseille. But this so-called broken language of ours was a choice of language, not of "understanding." It's possible to perform at least 25 languages on stage, and still not be able to express and subvert a language. I am immediately skeptical — and, unfortunately, always later proven right — of that actor who, instead of misplacing his own predictable language, is tempted to mislead others and himself, by overacting the nothingness that should be left unspoken (or spoken, which is the same thing).

Thank God, the 11th performance was "eventful" with the help of women from the gallery, who, crazed housewives lacking in Islamic manners, were scrambling eggs *&* chalk on the proscenium, with the other people in the audience hurling insults at them. The curtain fell. Delirium. But beware, this gallery of women's "revolt" is amusing, ah, ah, Simone (Beauvoir, of course, that great bungler from Camus to Sartre). It's amusing, since however you look at it, it's the removal of culinary assiduousness. What were they throwing from the gallery (the bass tuba swallowed two egg yolks)? Eggs and flour, ingredients, food and so on, overcooking. These women are bored with the kitchen. Cooking is the artist's diversion. It's a matter of measuring ingredients, it's well-known feminine unthinking, inaccessible to whoever is (not) only a woman.

These ladies use their pots and pans as mirrors, all the while meditating on their unintentional liberation; and if the dinner gets ruined? What do you want from them?

What I wouldn't give to just stay at home, away from the dull and grey din, the one wearing the pants. I can't count the number of times I cooked on stage. Courthouses, castles, stressful and desolate Americas, Kafka relived them all in the domestic sphere: obscene, and not common, tolerating the revival of servitude in the kitchen that male political intolerance had filled the women's ears with on the eve of every plebiscite... Parody & Greek stature, and not the warmed up, squawking male voices that our actresses, careless cooks, use to torment a pleasant summer's eardrums.

Woman (the feminine refusal to regress) is the infinite culinary carelessness of the universe.

Woman attempts to find the male in herself, the *ad hoc* cook, gone with the wind that emancipates, that emancipates.

Womanly is the neglected kitchen that, alas, così fan tutte, they serve you overcooked and cold in the proverbial predictable bed.

So, Michel Foucault invites me to dinner, *chez lui*, and he's doing the cooking. He's proud of it. And what a great cook he is!

After dinner, relaxing on the sofa, what do we do now, what do we do now? Do we ponder pensive speech? Do we dredge up the extraordinary "universal history of madness"? Not at all. Every conversation is a conversation for women. We sip our drinks without a care in the world, and that's all. Foucault compliments my splendid women's fishnet stockings that have red roses above the garters, my stage undergarments that I wore under the rancid green of the austere policeman's costume spotted with traces of Vaseline as if from a lordly orgasm. We move around a little, just enough to chase away the sight of the surprisingly few books; to pour ourselves another drink, a natural further confirmation that, simulated movements aside, "stability — everyone knows it — your name is woman!"

ANOTHER ONE HAMLET LESS

> But older age is Rome, demanding
> From actors not a gaudy blend
> Of props & reading, but in earnest
> A tragedy, with tragic end.
>
> B. Pasternak

A wonderful "portrait of the artist as a young man," no doubt about it. An umpteenth return to an Elsinore of the travelling wardrobes-chests for a static journey. Closer to Laforgue. The will of power (Shakespeare) par excellence offers-suffers himself. Though how much (& which) urgency is there in this missing "the dearest trains."

"Authentic" is "to recreate originally," Foscolo, impeccably, noted somewhere.

"To revisit" and so forth, but no. The Will (perhaps also William) can't stand anymore of the will.

I'm sitting here thinking about how to leave it behind de-finitively. To stop dreaming of "actresses' & princesses'" martyrdoms. It's true that a *hommelette* is one of my past futures. In short, it is necessary that it occur *without taking place*.

It will certainly not be another shaking of will to foil the awkward occasion of the empty event.

Beyond those doubts that have perpetually afflicted him, Hamlet, dressed in black, is a Baphomet turned on his head in the heroic refusal of those things that will take place.

Mortified and portrayed "from life," in a Romantic tabard, indiscipline in 5 acts, disguised as theatrical interdisciplinarity, this Gramatica's little production is versed in the bard's "rough English language"; as a demerit, this little production de-merits.

Damn that Œdipus who predicts them all, even "the things that are not." Driven out of Colonus-buen retiro, this blind old man put on his reading glasses. It is tedious violence. If then the transplant of the crystalline lens goes awry (Deleuze-Guattari are nevertheless courageous sawbones) that does not prevent other pharmacist scribes from attempting that experiment on *oblivion* and on *voice* again.

"Daddy, go ahead and try to yell at me, and you'll see what happens to (you) me!" Ah, yes, it is sickening to persist in such a post-Freudian pluri-placated, petty provocation, like an adjunct lectureship on the "cult of snow": mothers, whether they're whores or not, father assassins or victims, bureaucracy, families, institutions. To the convent, to the convent! If Kafka — lucky him — plays and is pleased with the contemptible world of law, Handi-Kapped, it is interesting because the game he plays (his writing) is *obscene*, derisory, ridiculous in the saying, and, even he, the author sneered at reading it.

The putrefied boat of love, "without (death) Zazà we can't stay," neck and ass shards where it pleases him most to rub himself (you cannot free yourself from your freedom, etc.).

Freedom, I never even attempt it myself; it doesn't interest me. These are knots that I loosen in the manner of the Macedonian. With respect to my way of thinking, Speak *&* Spell.

But let's get back to the *hommelette* that we are not. Let's return to our "'Bibi,' an abbreviation of Billy, and a diminutive of William."

Will no longer wants his Shake. What does that mean? Well, it is the saying that doesn't want it, it has no will (will = doublesexed, will = to want, will = desire, power = shakespeare):

> Get dressed, I don't give a fuck about my throne.
> Get dressed, I say!
> The dead are dead.
> We'll see the world. Paris.
> And now, my life, I'll show you!

This is will, plain and simple, they'll say. But, of course, it is will, but, in the meantime, it is will to get out of there. N.B.: Paris doesn't exist.

Hamlet is therefore *uninspired will*. Just look at that party of worms in Schopenhauer-Yorick's coffin.

Uninspired on stage? No doubt about it, my dear ladies: we abandon theater. But that's enough (I'm talking to myself) with this method of dismantling. Period. We don't mount a damn thing. Mounting the will *unwilled* of his very own will.

>   an equestrian will for his whole life
>   definitively anchored.

And the eternal-return? It does not return. We'll have to do without it, for once. *Visually* without it. Narcissus in perspective? Absolutely not: *pornography*, pierced (in its nice and ready holes) by the voice. A concert *quid*. What matters is that the saying does not stumble into visionary traps; that, deprived of the sexes, of the identico's erotic conflict, the image does not run the risk of constituting itself, ambiguous, as a referent to the word. Yes, I would like to taste an "hommelette" where unthinking allows Our Lady Naming to distract herself elsewhere, with her back to the obscene.

"Oh God, oh God, what a lack of moral sense!" Lærtes will say in reply (and in replying we can only speak nonsense), not at all scandalized by his obscene being, on display.

And I say, what a lack of theatrical sense! That is why we will tolerate Horatio-will-no-shake, for the sole purpose of irritating him and amusing the plebs with him showing off and grandstanding rather than performing.

Let's not Shake up a damn thing this time. An indecorous scene, apart from the travelling wardrobes-chests for a static journey; having rented the organza dresses from *Giselle* (they're lighter) from the award-winning Sartoria Farani, we'll be gone with the wind to more than four or five of the "best paid stages," to squander the umpteenth season of our flash-in-the-pan life.

Hamlet, or the non-history of waste ("hommelette"), the Freudian *côté* entrusted to the obscene good looks of a very beautiful young woman disguised as Polonius, wearing his foolish-white beard.

We'll sing without following the music,

> as if we were there in the other room,
> as if we were no longer us;
> and, above all, we will not work, do you hear us?
> We will not work.
> And we will never be able to die.

"Let death die!" yes, the battle cries that the great Tamerlano shouts when he finds himself short of enemies.

One more will, the last one, listless, is just what I need to go beyond Western "erotic civilization"; the duty to be an artist as well. This last will is like the typical restlessness of the dead. Estrangement. In our own incomprehension. Beyond alternative suffering. The emergency room of the insane asylum that excludes us once and for all, is to stop the image in whatever state of scandalous fixity, is to stop it in its flat design exonerated by the curves that insinuate desire, even if parodied, without Faustian regrets for obstinate youth, open-mouthed in the face of belligerent history. The last will for this pornographic non-state, in an anti-erotic-civilized refuge: anti-civilized disappearing-telling in the fairytale of amnesia. Let the last will be this *démaquillage* of the pensive-delusional face of the will that we are.

Do you remember? Toothless, you were smiling at your own provisional smile lying on the small glass table in the dentist's office. You thought that you, too, were that inanimate overcoat on the reclining chair, forgotten by who knows who.

Then there was that morning. It was a Sunday. Back at the dentist's office: the mechanic with your smile in his pocket was taking a long time. He finally turned up, but it would have been better if he hadn't, because when he appeared and pulled from his pocket your long-perfected porcelain expression, among the many he had in there, he dropped it — the scoundrel!

— shattering it into pieces on the hard floor. "Why don't you put carpet in your offices?" you swore like a troglodyte to Asclepius, who was nodding with I no longer remember what borrowed face. *Alas, poor Yorick!*

The last will to make a pittance to allow yourself the luxury of not having to perform every night, and to turn in to watch over your ruin, after having lost your best friends — *"généreux jusqu'au vice"*; a vampire, alone with your serenade to madness, an old, faithful rag curled up in a corner. That's enough of will.

A smile is nothing to laugh about.

OEDIPUS THE ACTOR

> When I look at a child: how shameful *&* stultifying
>   is the yoke it will bear,
> its suffering in seeking out others
> — as we seek them out — its search — like our own
>   — for truth, for beauty;
> when I think of its struggle withering away,
> that it will be alone, as we are!...
> Tear your sons from their cradles
> and cast them into the sea. Spare them
> from your ignominy!
>
> F. Hölderlin

How Freud succeeded in getting himself hung up in "Œdipus" remains a mystery to me to this day. The original clearly states — "pity" and "fear," which are indisputable conditions for the "tragic" — that "evil" is the end of "ignorance"; that the hero's hard-won "identity" transforms, on account of the notions on the *same*, the unhappy daily grind in an atrocious *vision*, enough to tear out your own eyes. What is this captured vision in Œdipus?

In the text: the assassin of his own father and, above all, the terrifying, recidivist, *maternity* we find in Jocasta, an obsessive matrix of life.

It is the life that she, a mother, disposes of, the life expelled by the female-queen; it is the birth, therefore, the condemnation of every Œdipus.

We cannot read the grandiose simplicity of *Œdipus Rex* without Sophocles' other eye, half-closed in *Œdipus at Colonus*.

"An author always does the same thing," Pier Paolo Pasolini never got tired of telling me, over and over again. Each one of his works cannot be considered a mosaic tile "apart" from the whole; it is not a member of its dismembered creator. No, the author is in his fullness in all his works. I know that I'm spouting "banalities" (but not really). We are born and, once we stop pitying that occurrence, we start to grow uneasy, in order to saddle life with some kind of *sense* that life simply does not have. We make plans, some of us for our own future (see Macbeth), and others of us, so as to ruin ourselves at all costs, for the past (Œdipus). I said: "so as to ruin ourselves," to see clearly, and off we go from one presumption to a more lethal one. Remember Othello, "I had been happy [...] so I had nothing known."

What sickens me is the clichéd inveighing against the father. What crime would Laïus have ever committed before his son murdered him? He attempted to make up for his own royal paternity; he tried to undo what his wife's whorish nature served up to this world. (Never mind the oracles who, like in Shakespeare, are pretexts for the mind's "plots.") In that sense, Tiresias, who "can no longer speak, but can sing incomprehensible words," is Œdipus's Colonus, his future-vanishing.

Paternity does not exist. "No one is a father to another," Œdipus says in Morante's *Serata a Colono*; precisely. It is that the furious arrogance of the ill-fated "I" (in all of us) becomes decidedly and paternally in charge of our "own" actions as soon as our father dies. This is when the delirium of feeling like your own father sets in, when you are "comforted" by no longer being a son, since your father is dead.

It would be useless to make *Œdipus* into a "mystery." His author knows everything. If it were a "mystery," with all the cards on the table, no one would read it anymore, no one would go to the theater to see it anymore.

Here is the absurd argument: my father is dead, now I'm no longer anyone's son; now I must *know*, I must "responsibly" prepare for my present-future. I must somehow take myself out of the equation. Will there be someone in charge of this communal plague? Well, if there is, then that enemy must be *removed*. Then he'll discover that he is himself "that enemy." *Naturally*.

Then will the torment shred itself: where is it hiding? And, not content with failing to find it (imagine it) in his own present, he starts to rummage senselessly through his past, until he gets to his birth: his mother who, a nonchalant criminal, calls a time-out on the love games with the "stranger," her husband-no-longer-lover, to entertain herself with a little phallus that is "all her own," this time to nurse and to raise; absent-minded. Then one fine day when this phallus is all grown up, she need only find a second distraction to get herself another one that will be "all her own." That's life. Whore. Matrix. Unthinking, she brings thoughts into this world that quickly become nightmares due to the cruel lashings of "identity."

Jocasta has committed no "crimes." She is *the* crime. And the crime is innocent.

But isn't it grotesque, ridiculous, beastly, this "respect" for maternity? These Madonnas with child, fucked or not.

The female expels us (Groddeck clearly saw that) from her womb. She abandons us to life's fair. If ever "hate" were to exist, well, let's reward the woman by calling her a "whore." How so? We know about this unpunished, congratulated bringing into the world of other people's mothers as "recounted." Of our own mother, Jesus Christ, we *are* certain: here we are. Everyone points the finger at daddy, when "mommy" is the cesspool from whence "we come."

Every maternity is a crime. It engenders monsters. It is the feminine sleep that reproduces, cruel-eternal, the reason *&* its ghosts.

No one (or almost no one) kills his own mother. Instead we celebrate her on "Mother's Day." Oh madhouses!, but isn't it "mommy" who "sent us to meet our maker"?

The cult of maternity is the blindest, most aberrant alienation of humankind. This our alienated way of bestowing "dignity" onto the misshapen smirk of which we consist. It is not true that this cruel inhuman matrix is the mother of God. God does not exist. It is man's matrix, and, what is more, we celebrate it. Its arrogance is an infinite absconding of our "being there."

If we were to knock it off its paltry altar, once and for all, then this "crime" would come back to play among us, returned to the obscene of exceeded desire. It would come back an "object" among the rest of us miserable "objects," and it would be done with the "visions."

Plummeted to earth, everyone is the actor of his "very own" anxiety.

But, having been twice a son to his whorish mother, whoever has made *actor* his profession must feel nauseous at every tickling of "identity."

Instead, what does that actor on stage do? He adores his mother, *and he believes it* to such an extent that he is capable of changing into an "other," night after night. Is this a parody of the "being there"? Not even in your wildest dreams (unless involuntary).

The actor *is there twice*, and it is this, ineffable, the umpteenth confirmation that he is usually twice as stupid as common human beings who are unintentional actors in their alienating daily toil.

   ... To never have been born, or just born
   to quickly return there where we were before.

Do you want me back, mommy? Tell me you've reconsidered.

TO JULES LAFORGUE

Woman will save the world. She will disperse the electric vapors of late summer's Pessimism with her terrestrial smile. Man is dead, long live Woman! She believes in the moi; she does not fear death, and she is blind to metaphysical anguish and to the distress of the unknowable. She is a happy life — Her inalienable and unchanging vocation, her reason for being, is to perpetuate life. The time for Woman's Reign has come — Man's function will now be art and to make his companion a mother. The day when, after centuries of Female History, woman arrives at pessimism, the world can commit suicide.

J. Laforgue (too young)

Alas, poor Jules!, what Woman's reign is he talking about? Certainly not the reign of the immobile queen — the "soi" blind to "metaphysical anguish" — if only that were the case. Here, we have the reign of woman's wardrobes that has collapsed on us. "It could not have ended but thus after having (she) rummaged around without rhyme or reason in *your* library." It is the reign of absent-minded mothers who shake off that "unique guilt" in the form of *life*, for which we have always been able to insult them. You see, Jules, these women, today, are all full of "metaphysical anguish," they are all disguised as despair of the "unknowable."

Did you notice how the "eternal feminine" that you were joking about does not know how to, nor can she, smile?

I know, you were too young when you wrote this little comment. Your aversion to the Parisian male permitted you to even take apples for oranges, absolutely. And, for that matter, your "bachelorhood" overpowered, with irony (self-irony), this your first-posthumous aforementioned confidence.

Jules, these women today suffer (they do not offer themselves). They are always nervous about absolutely nothing (and it's not all that important), possessed by the quotidian tran(s)vestism of cheap males. That "optimism" is not homemade. It is the woeful industrial fair of progress.

They killed their queen, these bees of bitterness (it still sounds sweet). Indeed, they even lost the "atrociousness" that makes them matrixes of filthy life, the one of "metaphysical" psychoses. C.B. assures you this much: he, compared to you, adorable misogynist, is nothing less than *Notre Dame des femmes*, so very saddened is he by the "evolution." The market, even the market refuses them. The dick market that they dream of subverting. We always make jokes about tragedies; never mind what we'll do with the ones to come:

TO JULES LAFORGUE

> T'occupe pas, sois Ton Regard,
> et sois l'âme qui s'exécute;
> tu fournis la matière brute,
> je me charge de l'œuvre d'art.

Well done, it's poetry. But the problem lies elsewhere. It's that we can't joke with the joke. It's an upper-lower-smile that cancels out the other.

"A happy life"? Don't you see that there's very little to be happy about. These women wear a frown. With respect to "life," no one was ever able to understand to the same extent as you were that "happiness" was elsewhere. Where it is no longer life.

> Quand reviendra l'automne
> Cette saison si triste,
> Je vais m'la passer bonne,
> Au point de vue artiste.

The artist, yes, keeps on boozing it up. Between one model and another, both of them absent.

"Life is a piece of shit, and you are my life!" Totò would say, casting a dirty look at the love of his life. These sound like your verses. There's no way out of it, not even if they dress poorly to displease "men," and to please the anguish found at the flea market.

I'll say it again, Jules, irresponsible and permanently damaged, they even lost the crime of being mothers. Don't you understand? They are daughters, *filles*, young girls-mothers with their "brains in their heads"; like at Cottolengo. And male optimism crushed them into a fake pessimism.

Art, yes, you can put your mind at ease: it "gets by," between rasping breaths *&* bad verses, but it refrains, I assure you, it refrains from impregnating a female. Art is terrified — and it's about time — to express itself.

P.S. In spite of "feminine history" having "arrived at (parodied) pessimism," "the world" has no intention of "committing suicide."

Yours truly

"RICHARD III" OR ON WORLDLY CRIME

It's strange, but not all that strange. In an actor's "ugly and beautiful" life, *Macbeth*'s ruin is always preceded by difference in *Richard III*.

In the masturbatory practice — the glans a martyr — it is as if it were written in the ogling sky, made a whore by myriad Shakespearean stars, that the Duke of Gloucester (later Richard III), a perverted horizontal politician, would plot with his damp mouth and hands the "noblest" erection of the Scottish king.

Even the majority of philologists — their pens dipped in hemorrhoidal holes — played a little sodomy game on the ascendant of York under the full banner of the lord of Glamis-Cawdor-Macbeth.

Even in the poetry that resulted from it, the poor, misled studies — we must admit — intuited that there's verse and then there's verse, that there's quantity and then there's quality, and that there's crime and then there's crime. So, there's blood and then there's blood: such that William's Will-phallus, a sovereign expert of holes — let's call them holes of being — allowed itself a few years to rub against the experience of an "English history," in order to merit a fine verticality (even verse is more rigid, essential, in Scotland's glans), to destroy Theophrastus's Indian tree.

Here you'll want to follow me with your dick in your hand, your finger wherever it pleases you, but undressed, ad-agio (slowly, musically speaking).

It was my turn to play Richard, now five years ago, when I was politely invited to conquer the Rocca Malatestiana fortress in Cesena, with a month for rehearsals. Oh, what conduct — I'm referring to my own! — if it produced white-colored blood (Albana wine a little "on the sweet side," and that's not good).

That different king assumed his role on stage — and on the streets — all tangled up in monstrous artificial limbs, to seduce history's beautiful sleeping beauties, desirous of the big, big scepter (regal in the sense of munificence), and he would gladly not give a damn about their lust, but he had to, it was his duty to belligerently immerse himself in the musky twists and turns of the underskirts of politics. Richard the glans would have to debase himself, if he truly intended to crown himself with nightmares.

I confessed, though I don't remember where, how the "political sphere" demeans me with regressive, beastly bliss. Mediocre ambition blinds me, it tickles me, it drips, it makes me, behind a feigned recommendation, a state-sponsored-member. There are those who, to avoid the sin of onanism, burden themselves with marrying someone who is not their woman-husband; and then there are others like me, who cannot amuse themselves if they don't do without it.

Power in an erotic perspective, the historical affair in an obscene illustration, are, at this point, long worn out notions, to bore to death a Catholic school girl from times past.

Let it be said for all to hear: my intransigent genius allows me, every now and again, an artistic vacation. I take the liberty, that is, to lower myself to an artist, only in those squawking socialites' cases that I find the most uninteresting & inane. It is the bitter pill in the form of a frog that, in the terrible games we played as children, we swallowed (*sic*) whole, because it is too disgusting to look at it. I swallowed a lot of those bitter frog pills, beyond the idiomatic expression.

"Blood for blood." Ah, yes, Albana wine from Emilia Romagna due to which, one day, exhausted, I stupidly extinguished a furnace of "human heat": that is, the clamorous charcoals in the bustling market below by pissing on them from the balcony of the Leon d'oro Hotel. Traffic cops, police. Arrest. "I was like a man on the farther shore / Of a stream" — still under the influence of that wine, when, as Tiresias, I menacingly prophesized that the local soccer team would end up in one of the lower leagues, which induced the inspired sergeant to temper my wrists with very nice handcuffs. I might get a pass for pissing on the market, but predicting that Cesena's team would be relegated to a lower league — anything but that — death to the astrologer.

It was a beautiful October midday. The police chief started to yell at me, not so much for the offence, as for having the same name as that C.B., the maestro and pride of the whole city, who, instead of pissing on good people, was at the Bonci Theater holding that very big Will in his hands, dumbass! Not to mention how I was disgracing the sacred name everyone was waiting for to come to the collective orgasm during what would be, without a shadow of a doubt, the first national evening of honor.

And it was Lydia who got me out of the non-existent mess I was in. How did she do it? Like this: she told him I was someone who didn't drink and was worn out from the "English" rehearsals, and taking a sip of Campari soda led to that calumny. She took care of exorcising me. A complete turnaround. The chief didn't know how, or to whom, he should apologize. The sergeant's accusations, yes, clearly, were overzealous and not at all diplomatic.

The city's assessor of culture, K., was mistaken about the maestro's bender and his exhaustion, because he believed in the most unbelievable breaths of my delirium: for example, of love put to the test *more uxorio* up until then, and that it was about time for the "heart's sigh" to be "solemnly blessed, and love commanded and made saintly, Godspeed" (and why not in Cesena, with a torchlight procession on the walls of the ages, the envy of men who lived in the countryside); farewell to our cultured reason for being there!

"RICHARD III" OR ON WORLDLY CRIME

The newspapers published the announcement, and the assessor got the whole council involved. In the space of a mere 48 hours, he had in his hands Lydia's documents and mine mixed in with his own personal documents — it was destiny, and I'll tell you why later.

"Maestro, when shall we perform the ceremony?"

"I need to rehearse. Now's not the time for jokes."

"Jokes, my foot! I bent over backwards to get the damned documents! Everything is ready, even the torches."

He was taking care of his city; no doubt about it: a legitimate marriage between two actors in Cesena wasn't something that happened every day. Once everything was ready, I changed my mind. About the bride: "I'm sorry, my friend, believe me, but there's been a horrible misunderstanding; a dreadful mix-up. I was planning to marry Susanna (Javicoli) and not Lydia."

So, K, that irreducible matchmaker, started all over again, with a practical & irrational faith, frenetically, at 10 frames a second.

"Here are the young woman's documents. Shall we say Sunday. This Sunday."

How to respond? We would be performing on Friday. He understood. Opening night was a success, and, finally in my dressing room, with the door closed and locked:

"You coward, it's you that I'm after!" I was about to kiss him, as out of reach as he was, not to mention as white as a ghost; there's "destiny" for you.

I awoke under glass, in a sunny stadium, a guest of Pasini, who is a really great guy. What was happening?

Cesena-Sampdoria: "We have Carmelo Bene here with us. Go ahead, tell us how it will turn out!"

"It'll be 3 to 0, for Cesena of course."

"Let's hope you're right. Look, Bene, you do know that Sampdoria is in first place in the rankings..."

"That means nothing. 3 to 0, I'm here."

The final score was 3 to 1 in favor of Cesena, with the 1000 spectators closest to me applauding me; like a center forward, incredulous, bewitched.

The halftime, however, yes, that was "mine." So, had it been decided that I would have to die in Cesena? "Where can I find a toilet, just to relieve myself," I asked. Good luck finding one; the toilets are down below, but you won't get through. A wall stood behind the spot where the commentator's booth was. A human wall of people, all of them on the tips of their toes, pushed up against it, figures glued to the wall — but where (?). There was a little spot, and I occupied it, with my back to the field. No one noticed anything; all eyes were on the field. But the concrete was at an incline, & the piss, as if having found its natural bed, flowed into poor Pasini's little booth. The antagonism on the field — Cesena had never been so unstoppable — saved me from the worst, since I would have been a repeat offender.

Like Lady Macbeth, I would see the red-white Albana wine of blood, "here's another damned spot." Everywhere, in the crowd's "massacre," and at the same time in the Fiorita Stadium's lofty azure. Oh,

> If the assassination
> could trammel up the consequence, and catch
> with his surcease success; that but this blow
> might be the be-all and the end-all here,
> but here, upon this bank and shoal of time,
> we'd jump the life to come.

"Oh, sight, oh horrible sight!" These anecdotes were pissing the parody of the tragedy on stage on themselves. And the zeal in miniature of the assessorial apprehension in loco, pantographed that other perversion of Richard-nonsense, born, indeed, to propitiate — by playing the assassin, and he, too, unfailingly threatened by the ghostly sheets on his bed — the Macbethian *noble phallus*.

A chain of seductions on the coffins of his very own victims, then abandoned by Lady-History, Richard plays at believing his own lies, lacerating, soliloquy, the fetishism of the garments abandoned on the stage of his solitude by that pig of a woman of his, who went off to get laid, who knows in which elsewhere, minimizing the spent and decrowned prick's alcoholic & insipidly combative plans, no longer a "worthy" consort:

> You're leaving, going abroad?...
> You'll discover lots of things to learn...

So, prescribed by chance, the music, an ugly slut, played on a mandolin was that Verdian *Macbeth*:

> The vanguard all spread out over the length!...
> I'll follow with the bulk of the army!...
> Saint George will provide reinforcements!...
> To hell with conscience!...

Here, you see: already "Ricciardetto" ("a knock on his noodle with the pommel of a dagger!... And then you drown him in a cask of Malmsey... And make soup!") had unhooded the Tamerlanian glans — in the space of only an hour of the play — of the political-social-conscience. Without fault and undamned from the derisory succession of events, he — mediumistic C.B. — produced himself in *saying the blood of the acting-suffering* (screams and silences and "precipitates"); when he no longer knows what he can ever promise Elisabeth, after the list of reigns, to take her daughter to bed:

"RICHARD III" OR ON WORLDLY CRIME

Well then tell her that I love her!

It is the sovereign scream (the most unlikely ploy and, for this reason, cried out), this cry of the "love" proffered by Richard, no longer different in the eyes of a political-extra-fucked mother. It is a Will who fucked me *comme il faut,* who fucked identity and fate up his ass; and a ringing from the throat was reverberating amidst the nausea as if from a return from the buttocks stung at full force, into the void of a full theater.

Richard does not show off as much as *Macbeth* does. Nevertheless, we should recall that these two kings are both innocent and good in Holinshed's *Chronicles.* I was performing at the Quirino when I learned that a certain Richard Society had won its "historical" case, and a London court had not only acquitted the Third York but also accepted its request to erect an equestrian monument in his honor, in reparation, sluggard-historic-Pinocchio, for the affronts with which the British bard had, who knows why, saddled that sovereign. That horse, which I was invoking in his place to vanish from the stage, would have been much more suited to Bosworth.

Therefore, *Richard III* and *Macbeth,* differing in two facts of more than a little significance: Macbeth is married, and the other is a bachelor.

If in terms of "quality," it is *Richard III* that is able to equip the Scotsman's most noteworthy member, in the *quantum* of the interior, of the domestic, it mustn't mislead by any means *copulation's privilege*; since in both histories, the true Lady, *masturbation*, is queen; in any event, the Scottish copulation is only its surrogate.

Every "respectable" *ménage* is necessarily complicity, though certainly not with respect to the furnishings and the grocery shopping. Complicity at its peak is crime. Every crime is a "love story." The contrary is not true, since not every love is evil-blessed by its acme. The bedrock of the "social good" is the absconding of the crime, and everyone, apart from certain cases, abides by it.

I believe there is such a "case," reported in Wilson's *Encyclopedia of Murder*:

It's always the same story, a tale of two lovers. She is a beautiful young widow, the mother of a little girl. The two of them "adore" each other, and then, one fine day, at his request, they dismember that blame(less) creature. The gallows for both of them. In the courtroom, on the day of their sentencing, she, dressed elegantly in the finest black, when passing in front of her partner (ladies first), drops a glove at his feet. Sublime vainglory.

What hadn't those two not done? They had mocked eternal life (sacrificing the little girl), to play at remorse, to play at that secret that only crime is able to — up to a certain point — safeguard. They had both given their life to the other, this life here on earth. And as if all that abandonment weren't enough, even the *end's* heroic *vainglory* is the end's vanity.

Let's Macbethize... From the universal stillness of the non-dead, once and for all, the regal half-sleep, the Duncan-historic body, allows itself to be titillated one fine morning by a cock-a-doodle-do. Then, unfortunate, he trades his ecstatic-sovereign mummy with the first senseless gesture that occurs to him. He rashly unravels the bandages of his immobility at the mercy of the "acting-suffering" that plummets him into *Macbeth* (his very own death, to start with). Macbeth, an absurd actor, continues Duncan's reign, and in life, he has tied the knot for good with a worthy love (a theater-worthy love): his woman-boy-Lady Macbeth.

So, gone with the wind, they love each other out of the *blood* that is suited *to the love that expresses itself*.

The two of them carry out an attack (Duncan's royal body is a simulacrum) on their own love, exciting each other in inviolable turns. They knock on their very own terror. These wonderful actors run out of breath from the perpetual search for a *self-fright* that mirrors the *auteur's feminine*.

They dress (they are dressed) and undress moods. Action is the *saying*, and *scene* the *imaginary*.

It is the clothing, the armor, the accessories of the odds and ends on stage that dictate the gestures, the movements & the voices, the song the laugh the tears, the very aphasia of the saying.

What about the feelings, and the soul? We have never licked a feeling. Never penetrated a soul. What can we do with them? We preserve these concerns about the spirit in spirits. They will make rancid preserves out of them from which — with a shortage on the horizon — they will continue to season the routine of the theater of "parroting."

Macbeth is a forfeiture of the stage. His wife, as written in the script, will abandon him at a certain point, and farewell, "the nurse for the love of art." And all that will remain to the Macbeth-body, denied even the marital bed, will be the forced day-to-day work on stage. A crazed labor beyond measure. From one armor to an even heavier one, and, therefore, the bed, with a small table at its head; the stupefying relocation that is life. To rip up the stage floor and overturn it with arms outstretched to the nothingness, in that

> Tomorrow, and tomorrow, and tomorrow,
> creeps in this petty pace from day to day...

The actor's obscene-heroic history:

In the beginning it is sleep, then it is half-sleep, followed by the action, with the "I" deluding itself about its author, and suffered in the saying, and then the reawakening of sense, out of place, in the child witches' *non-sense* games.

As if the temptation *of the being there* weren't enough for him to suffer shame, even predestined to..., prophesized by the "supernatural," he foolishly follows the plot. As if all of this were still not enough (were missing), here is the "guilty" glans, made responsible, never having felt an objective prompting kiss: because in murder no author exists who is the *same* a moment before and a moment after the "misdeed"; because, apart from telling ourselves that we are, we cannot be, assassins. Damnation is this innocence.

What remains is perversion: this life pitifully replaced by existence. Love, on the other hand, does not remain, if not among us disaffected, to play at the "little death." With respect to the Other death, it will come when everything is already dead. To gather the oblivion that we did not want and that we could not be.

That's it. A bandaged arm. A wound? So, unroll this bandage, unroll, unroll: white white less white a bit of red red red more red (is the lesion here?) Unroll unroll less red less red less red White white more white and gone is the bandage Nothingness.

Wounded was the bandage and not the arm.
Might this, *&* nothing else, be melancholy (?).

"MACBETH" OR THE SUNSET OF SOLITUDE

There's no doubt about it. Solitude is a pleasant companion. The end of life married to the frivolous talk of love. Well, yes, because these females do not intend to let themselves be, I won't say, invented — because for this there is no need to ask for their consent — they don't understand that there is nothing to understand. Woman is respite (or should be) from the daily grind of pensive male pride's little sins.

If I say "respite," it is, above all, in reference to the respite of the idea; of the senseless chomping at the bit outside the coffin: the great amount of daily grief experienced by the "I" that feels presumptuous life as a premature burial. Grotesque anxiety.

These indignant females, therefore, disregard the beyond happiness of the mere object. They busy themselves impatiently, going from one impulse to the next, shaken from the identity that would have them be mad.

But let's get back to us, the remains. How many people deceive themselves into believing that, having broken all ties to the world, a table well-laid for fasting is ready for them, the chosen ones, away from the human crowd. Is, for example, the hermit, far from the much talked-about world, alone? And what about faith, rancor, or the misconceived love of God, the little aspiration to climb the ladder to heaven, the well-earned misogyny, etc., yes, these misunderstandings of his subject-malaise, where did they go? They are there, in his mental baggage, which he carried with him. They are within him. They are *him*. It would have been better had he done the opposite, when he was focused on the preparations for his trip. That is, had he left himself in society and brought all of society with him, he could now, in this comical little theater, feign the humors, like people used to do in the last century. The irony of those daily forced labors, who knows, in certain moments of detachment, of abandon, would, perhaps, have amused him a little. But, instead, now he has to seriously endure those ghostly humors of his; and bite his fingernails at the dark thought:

Nothing exists except that which is not.

It is he, wretched, who is overcrowded. He talks to himself, with a loud and a soft voice. He *is* there. Perhaps he is tempted to draft an autobiography in his own blood. Even if imaginary. He's there in three ways: as a memory of his worldly behavior; as his current state, emptied of his sense of humor; and lastly, as the hallucinatory unknown (I'm clearly dealing with "European solitudes").

It is, therefore, that solitude that he should have left at home, without necessarily leaving home.

As for me as an actor, this year I am subtracting *Macbeth* from the stage. It was about time. But the fact is that we cannot plan certain operations, in this way, at random. Why not? Because Macbeth is *the hero annihilated by his own plan.*

Macbeth is not a play among the others. We can only be Macbeth if our brain is deprogrammed. We cannot program the resetting of ourselves to zero at our leisure. On the contrary, it will have been necessary to go through life with cutting blows; to confront thus the un-happy consciousness, to encounter Madonna Solitude, and, in the end, having bid farewell to this lady, *lose our minds* definitively. "Lose our minds," so we become accustomed to disparaging crazy people. I am close to that point, because solitude is no longer my companion, and I am truly starting *"to grow weary of the sun."*

Like a Thracian gladiator in the Sahara's arena, with women and friends as absent spectators, and the all too many things that "await," I look exactly like that Herod Antipas of mine, moving around senselessly the pink and blue pieces carved in ice on the chessboard, between the intermissions and the feigned beating of his heart, desirous — he feigns his urges as well — while waiting — he feigns waiting as well — for the childish life in Salome to please him among the veils dancing the invisible. An extreme parody of the game and of the plan, because kings queens bishops rooks melt in his hands, in the delayed sequence of the moves — the reflections are feigned as well — in a cold puddle of water.

And Antipas checkmates himself king.

> Salome, dance for me,
> What do I care if she dances or not!

"... And do not fear the destruction, for these things must happen first, but the end will not come at once," as it says somewhere in the Gospels. For André Gide, eternity begins in this very life, at the moment of your "redemption." Lucky him. From my time as a young man during which I sought the end of theater, here I am, at the theater of the end. What an apprenticeship, this one of unlearning. Is our own birth not, perhaps, a distraction in another kind of urge?

> Hé pas choisi
> D'y naître, et hommes!
> Mais nous y sommes,
> Tenons-nous-y.

We are born. After that, life seems to be the time accorded to the grotesque justification of the being there. In fact, even good people with common sense "kill time."

Of course, they do. There's that old adage that says, "then it all starts over again." Indeed, it starts over again, but from the end, like the dead come before the living, in Freud's best work.

Macbeth ("Handsome and Ugly," it makes no difference!) will be the end of every theater of the possible. "You're as caustic as ever!" You'll see, if you have the ear for it. It is that we are impudent and stupid: as soon as we're born, we all start crying, (no) doubt about it. What is it that makes us cry? The regretted future. And the end. The end that enlivens us. Whoever decides to start drinking, should go ahead and drink. I knocked back all of Scotland, diluting my "I" in the glass, swallowing "the speaking" and re-vomiting myself up as *an object*. My stomach has always rejected my soul. This is how people can drink without being drunk, like, in contrast, what happens to the majority of abstainers. Enough of art, this is where genius begins. Then the journalistic sneer doesn't leave a trace: the events' illusory information. Culture is ignorance, just as the end is its own beginning. The sadness for the things that never had a beginning puts the smile of the dead on the closed silence of the lips, and it sings incomprehensible the voice of the listening.

What has been? Not a damn thing. Let's say we played at frightening ourselves, knocking from the inside; at imagining a specter of fear, a remorse to keep us company. Dressed in the most varied of humors, to persuade ourselves that it is we who decide our gestures. Then, like how the suit doesn't make the man, when the habit is tired of its monk, the monastery disappears, uninhabited.

The definitively non-dead's pathetic restlessness finds its inanimate existence safeguarded from the tickling of historical recycling.

I want to disinter myself; I mistrust the bandaged stillness as a mummy. That whore, fortune, is also bandaged. I mistrust the however much Pharaonic exposure time. I am an actor, and the last curiosity, you'll understand, is to verify my regression.

Let's resurrect it. Then this tired masterpiece of embalming will dissolve. Enough of resuscitating every day! The miracle's routine is too stressful. Even eternity has its Bartlebys.

Perhaps I have told you very little. It is what I was able to imagine. But is it not precisely what is missing that matters in life?

How many trifles I would have spared you, had I been in this world and had God existed.

ACKNOWLEDGMENTS

It is rare for translations to have soloists-sorcerers singing their wordy ways across languages. Translations require a chorus of voices from both source and target languages if they hope to render compositions that carry the music of the original and the tenor of the target language text. In the present case of translating Carmelo Bene, it required an orchestra.

This translation project was born from love. It was my (then future) husband who introduced me to Bene's work in our budding relationship. Thus, I fell in love twice in a fairly short time. First with Alessio Andronico, and then with Bene, though in different ways. The project, which was dreamt up over a decade ago, and became a real thing in the world many years later, would not have been possible without the support of my loving husband, both the sustaining support of an attentive spouse and the intellectual support of an astute native speaker of Italian, not to mention a careful reader of English. I thank him for his many contributions.

This project would also not have been possible, were it not for my editor, my friend, Rainer J. Hanshe, and his dogged determination to publish Carmelo Bene in English. I would like to thank him, above all, for his persistence and encouragement, but also for his passion to see this project born in a world that needs more voices like Bene's, for his keen eye, and for his wordcraft.

I would like to give special thanks to my former teacher and constant friend, Marco Codebò, for reading my translations against the Italian. His cultural knowledge is vast, such that his interventions allowed the translation to capture the nuances of Bene's world.

I would also like to thank the many Italian speakers who contributed to my understanding of the texts and of Bene's life: Carlo Alberto Petruzzi, for his very close reading; Luisa Viglietti, for sharing with me her story of the years she spent with Bene before he died; Pierpaolo Tondini and Elio Paiano, for their hospitality in Otranto and for sharing anecdotes about Bene during the years he lived there; Signora Sticchi, for her generosity in allowing me to visit with her in the Moorish villa that figures in I Appeared to the Madonna and which appears as a setting in his literary and film versions of *Nostra Signora dei Turchi*.

COLOPHON

I APPEARED TO THE MADONNA
was handset in InDesign CC.

The text font is *Skolar*.
The display font is *Labil Grotesk*.

Book design & typesetting: Alessandro Segalini
Cover image: Federico Gori
Cover design: Alessandro Segalini & CMP

I APPEARED TO THE MADONNA
is published by Contra Mundum Press.

CONTRA MUNDUM PRESS

Dedicated to the value & the indispensable importance of the individual voice, to works that test the boundaries of thought & experience.

The primary aim of Contra Mundum is to publish translations of writers who in their use of form and style are *à rebours*, or who deviate significantly from more programmatic & spurious forms of experimentation. Such writing attests to the volatile nature of modernism. Our preference is for works that have not yet been translated into English, are out of print, or are poorly translated, for writers whose thinking & æsthetics are in opposition to timely or mainstream currents of thought, value systems, or moralities. We also reprint obscure and out-of-print works we consider significant but which have been forgotten, neglected, or overshadowed.

There are many works of fundamental significance to *Weltliteratur* (& *Weltkultur*) that still remain in relative oblivion, works that alter and disrupt standard circuits of thought — these warrant being encountered by the world at large. It is our aim to render them more visible.

For the complete list of forthcoming publications, please visit our website. To be added to our mailing list, send your name and email address to: info@contramundum.net

Contra Mundum Press
P.O. Box 1326
New York, NY 10276
USA

OTHER CONTRA MUNDUM PRESS TITLES

2012 *Gilgamesh*
      Ghérasim Luca, *Self-Shadowing Prey*
      Rainer J. Hanshe, *The Abdication*
      Walter Jackson Bate, *Negative Capability*
      Miklós Szentkuthy, *Marginalia on Casanova*
      Fernando Pessoa, *Philosophical Essays*
2013 Elio Petri, *Writings on Cinema & Life*
      Friedrich Nietzsche, *The Greek Music Drama*
      Richard Foreman, *Plays with Films*
      Louis-Auguste Blanqui, *Eternity by the Stars*
      Miklós Szentkuthy, *Towards the One & Only Metaphor*
      Josef Winkler, *When the Time Comes*
2014 William Wordsworth, *Fragments*
      Josef Winkler, *Natura Morta*
      Fernando Pessoa, *The Transformation Book*
      Emilio Villa, *The Selected Poetry of Emilio Villa*
      Robert Kelly, *A Voice Full of Cities*
      Pier Paolo Pasolini, *The Divine Mimesis*
      Miklós Szentkuthy, *Prae, Vol. 1*
2015 Federico Fellini, *Making a Film*
      Robert Musil, *Thought Flights*
      Sándor Tar, *Our Street*
      Lorand Gaspar, *Earth Absolute*
      Josef Winkler, *The Graveyard of Bitter Oranges*
      Ferit Edgü, *Noone*
      Jean-Jacques Rousseau, *Narcissus*
      Ahmad Shamlu, *Born Upon the Dark Spear*

2016	Jean-Luc Godard, *Phrases*
	Otto Dix, *Letters, Vol. 1*
	Maura Del Serra, *Ladder of Oaths*
	Pierre Senges, *The Major Refutation*
	Charles Baudelaire, *My Heart Laid Bare & Other Texts*
2017	Joseph Kessel, *Army of Shadows*
	Rainer J. Hanshe & Federico Gori, *Shattering the Muses*
	Gérard Depardieu, *Innocent*
	Claude Mouchard, *Entangled — Papers! — Notes*
2018	Miklós Szentkuthy, *Black Renaissance*
	Adonis & Pierre Joris, *Conversations in the Pyrenees*
2019	Charles Baudelaire, *Belgium Stripped Bare*
	Robert Musil, *Unions*
	Iceberg Slim, *Night Train to Sugar Hill*
	Marquis de Sade, *Aline & Valcour*
2020	Rédoine Faïd, *Outlaw*
	A City Full of Voices: Essays on the Work of Robert Kelly
	Paul Celan, *Microliths*

SOME FORTHCOMING TITLES

Zsuzsa Selyem, *It's Raining in Moscow*
Oğuz Atay, *While Waiting for Fear*

THE FUTURE OF KULCHUR
A PATRONAGE PROJECT

LEND CONTRA MUNDUM PRESS (CMP) YOUR SUPPORT

With bookstores and presses around the world struggling to survive, and many actually closing, we are forming this patronage project as a means for establishing a continuous & stable foundation to safeguard our longevity. Through this patronage project we would be able to remain free of having to rely upon government support &/or other official funding bodies, not to speak of their timelines & impositions. It would also free CMP from suffering the vagaries of the publishing industry, as well as the risk of submitting to commercial pressures in order to persist, thereby potentially compromising the integrity of our catalog.

CAN YOU SACRIFICE $10 A WEEK FOR KULCHUR?

For the equivalent of merely 2–3 coffees a week, you can help sustain CMP and contribute to the future of kulchur. To participate in our patronage program we are asking individuals to donate $500 per year, which amounts to $42/month, or $10/week. Larger donations are of course welcome and beneficial. All donations are tax-deductible through our fiscal sponsor Fractured Atlas. If preferred, donations can be made in two installments. We are seeking a minimum of 300 patrons per year and would like for them to commit to giving the above amount for a period of three years.

WHAT WE OFFER

Part tax-deductible donation, part exchange, for your contribution you will receive every CMP book published during the patronage period as well as 20 books from our back catalog. When possible, signed or limited editions of books will be offered as well.

WHAT WILL CMP DO WITH YOUR CONTRIBUTIONS?

Your contribution will help with basic general operating expenses, yearly production expenses (book printing, warehouse & catalog fees, etc.), advertising & outreach, and editorial, proofreading, translation, typography, design and copyright fees. Funds may also be used for participating in book fairs and staging events. Additionally, we hope to rebuild the *Hyperion* section of the website in order to modernize it.

From Pericles to Mæcenas & the Renaissance patrons, it is the magnanimity of such individuals that have helped the arts to flourish. Be a part of helping your kulchur flourish; be a part of history.

HOW

To lend your support & become a patron, please visit the subscription page of our website: contramundum.net/subscription

For any questions, write us at: info@contramundum.net